"*Marcia is my personal Dream Coach® because she helps me think much bigger about what's possible and clarify what I want to accomplish. I could work with anyone but choose her because she is simply the best.*"

~**Jack Canfield,** Coauthor, *Chicken Soup for the Soul* Series and *Success Principles*

"*Marcia Wieder and I have been teaching about passion for many decades. When it comes to learning how to stand in your purpose to create, discover and act on important dreams, she is in a class by herself. If you want to truly learn how to achieve your dreams from the best, look no further.*"

~**Janet Bray Attwood,** NY Times Best-Selling Author, *The Passion Test*

"*In business, our ability to have an inspired vision that we can act upon is crucial to success. Marcia Wieder understands that dreaming and envisioning our own ideal future is a 'whole brain' process, and her insightful new book provides a solid methodology for being both visionary and practical. Marcia's work is in a league of its own, and I cannot recommend this book more highly.*"

~**Ivan Misner,** Ph.D., NY Times Best-Selling Author, *Masters of Networking* and Founder, BNI®

"*All of the great business success in the modern era began with a dream. Dreams are what motivated every successful entrepreneur I've ever studied or known. Marcia's incredible book is more than an inspiration piece; it is a manual for how to grasp what you are passionate about and then ground it into reality. In that sense, her book is more than just about dreams—it's about creating the world we choose for ourselves rather than the one we incorrectly believe we must accept. It is absolutely correct that 'dreams do come true,' provided, like Marcia, you have the technology and determination to pursue them until they arrive. Thank you, Marcia for writing a great book about human nature, and in the process writing one of the best business textbooks at the same time!*"

~**Rinaldo S. Brutoco,** Founding President/CEO, World Business Academy

"In her newest book DREAM, *the amazing Marcia Wieder gives you the total gift of confidence to break through ANY thing that might stop you. She also instills full awareness of the specific steps that take your dream from simply an idea to becoming the essence of the life you love living. If you follow the code in this book, it will change your life for good, forever."*

~**Mary Morrissey**, Best-Selling Author,
Building Your Field of Dreams, Founder, Life Mastery Institute

"If you want to dream a new project, a new life, or even a new world into 3D reality, Marcia will show you how in the most elegant way possible (as she has for me). In DREAM, *she illuminates the key steps to clearing out the past, harnessing the rocket fuel of your passion, and blasting off into the stratosphere of unlimited possibility, a realm occupied by history's biggest dreamers. She combines a playful spirit with straight talk that pares away our excuses, doubts and fears to reveal the vivid clarity of our soul. Marcia shows us that we are each here to birth our dreams and when we do, the world will never be the same!"*

~**Stephen Dinan**, CEO, The Shift Network

"There is no one better than Marcia Wieder to help you turn your dreams into a reality. I have personally worked with Marcia over the last twenty years, and her principles have helped me achieve many lifelong dreams, including writing a best-selling book, building a successful business and now running a humanitarian organization that is deeply meaningful to me. DREAM *is a powerful guide filled with practical information that will inspire you to dream bigger than you ever thought possible and live a life of purpose and meaning."*

~**Cynthia Kersey**, Best-Selling Author, *Unstoppable*,
And Founder/CEO, Unstoppable Foundation

"Marcia is a master at helping you get real clarity about what you want and how to get it. Her amazing process will guide you in achieving your personal or professional dreams faster."

~**Sandra Yancey**, Founder/CEO of eWomenNetwork

"To some, dreams are far up in the clouds and unattainable; to Marcia, they are full of possibility and potential. If anyone can help you reach your dreams, she can."

~**Adam Markel**, CEO, New Peaks

"If you are reading these words, take it as proof that your dreams can come true. Marcia Wieder, the Queen of Dreams, is a master manifestor. In this book she shares everything you need to know to make it happen. Lucky you!"

~**Arielle Ford**, Author, *The Soulmate Secret*

"Reading this book will help you remember that a richer and more meaningful life begins with a deeper relationship with yourself."

~**Gerald Jampolsky**, MD, Founder,
Center for Attitudinal Healing

"With three decades of solid experience, Marcia Wieder continues to be a leader and innovator in the field of human potential. This powerful book is filled with her practical knowledge and inspiring examples, serving as the bible for achieving your dreams."

~**Doron Libshtein**, Founder/CEO, The Mentors Channel

"Many people have brilliant dreams. But tragically few turn them into reality. Why? Because they don't have a blueprint. But Marcia Wieder does. In this compelling book you'll find a practical, systematic, easy process to make your dreams come true. It's time to dream big!"

~**Christine Comaford**, NY Times Best-Selling Author,
SmartTribes and *Rules for Renegades*

"In his famous notebooks, Leonardo da Vinci wrote, 'Fix your course to a star' and 'I wish to work miracles.' Marcia Wieder is a world-class expert in helping you discover your guiding star. She inspires you to open your mind and heart to go beyond what you imagine is possible so that you can experience miracles in your life now. In DREAM, Marcia applies her genius to help you discover creative ways to manifest what is most important to you."

~**Michael J. Gelb**, Best-Selling Author, *How to Think Like Leonardo da Vinci* and *Creativity on Demand*

"*Marcia is the reigning queen of dreaming. This book articulates her most up-to-date methods, from decades spent helping hundreds of thousands of people find and live their dreams. It couldn't be more timely—there has never been more opportunity to live your dream. And with all the challenges society is facing, living your dream will be a magnificent contribution to others. Let Marcia be your guide to a new life and a new world.*"

~**Tim Kelley, Author**, *True Purpose* and Founder, True Purpose®Institute

"*DREAM encapsulates thirty years of wisdom and pragmatics that Marcia has amassed from coaching thousands of executives, entrepreneurs and visionaries to manifest their dreams. Its vital message will help take you home to your true calling, give you a step-by-step road map to unleashing your potential and then inspire you with your soul's greatest possibilities. DREAM is a not-to-be-missed, soon-to-be classic in the literature on creativity, manifestation and spirituality.*"

~**Amy Elizabeth Fox**, CEO, Mobius Executive Leadership

"*In DREAM, super mentor Marcia Wieder has produced an invaluable tool kit for creating the kind of life most of us only dream about. Among the countless gems contained in this book are three vital pieces of advice: tell the universe exactly what you want, maintain the belief that it is within reach and, most important of all, have the courage to act on the improbable. This book should come with a warning: may help you to reclaim your life.*"

~**Lynne McTaggart**, Best Selling Author, *The Intention Experiment* and *The Field*

"As a veteran filmmaker, I can tell you that billions of dollars are invested to convince us that we should feel, look and be a certain way. As a result, over the course of generations, we've lost touch with who and what we truly are. DREAM is a brilliantly accurate map and compass designed to realign you with your highest path and the life you were born to live."

~**Mikki Willis**, Founder, Elevate Films

"With deep wisdom and uplifting encouragement, Marcia teaches us how to actually make our dreams come true. This book is the guide for anyone who is ready to reconnect to their deepest desires and take an empowering step into who they truly are."

~**Christine Hassler**, Best-Selling Author,
Expectation Hangover

"It's one thing to have big dreams and quite another to manifest them. As an industry thought leader, Marcia Wieder is a respected expert in this field. In her groundbreaking new book DREAM she provides brilliant insights and practical shortcuts for creating a meaningful life."

~**Gay Hendricks**, Author, *The Big Leap and Conscious Loving*

"Marcia's creativity has inspired students worldwide to access practical tools in order to monetize their dreams and achieve real results quickly. This book is her finest work."

~**Raymond Aaron**, Best-Selling Author,
Double Your Income Doing What You Love

"The key to living a truly creative life is the power to envision and dream. One of the true masters of teaching this is Marcia Wieder. This book is a priceless gem I am proud to have on my shelf."

~**Barnet Bain**, Producer, What Dreams May Come, and
Author, *The Book of Doing and Being*

"*If you are finally ready to take focused action to live your dream life, then read Marcia's book. She provides practical tools and solid skills to discover your purpose and ignite passion, which will inspire you to create new dreams and turn the most important ones into reality.*"

~Katherine Woodward Thomas, Best-Selling Author
Conscious Uncoupling

"*Reading* DREAM *is like talking to your best friend. It is simple yet sophisticated, inspiring and encouraging—and it will cause you to take action. This is true even for someone like me, who teaches others how to make their dreams a reality.*"

~Yuval Abramovitz, Author, *The List: Shout Out Your Dreams!*

"*Marcia begins her book by saying, 'Dream is a verb.' Her life and her work are true examples of what dreams are made of. If you want to move your dreams from wish to reality, from thought to substance, get this book and follow its guidance religiously.*"

~Blaine Bartlett, Author, *Compassionate Capitalism* and CEO, Avatar Resources

"*Marcia's dream is that our dreams become a reality. She's taught many of us that the key to realizing our dreams is to put them into action. In this new and powerful book, she has distilled a lifetime of wisdom into a straightforward guide to being who we are and bringing ourselves and our potential into the world. This book is more than a compilation of self-help tips and techniques; it is a conversation with a master—a master of dreams and possibilities for who we can be IF we give ourselves permission to DREAM.*"

~Jim Selman, Founder, The Eldering Institute

"This powerful book guides us through the tender stage of dreaming, and the pitfalls we can experience in creating a dream. This well-crafted volume instructs in the art of creating what we aim for with unique strategies for success. DREAM is a book of great inspiration, courage, and hope; every word rings with truth and the beauty of what is ultimately possible for us all."

~**Debbi Dachinger**, Syndicated Media Personality and Best-Selling Author, *Dare to Dream*

"DREAM serves as far more than a guide or a how-to manual. It's more like a lifeline to inspiration. The masterful way in which Marcia weaves story after story through her narrative stirs the fire in your belly, makes you shed excuses like an ill-fitting coat. I was awestruck by how she honors each of us and moves us into action, calling us 'a perfect and exquisite expression of love masquerading as a human being.' Who doesn't feel superb about that—and, more importantly, motivated to become that? My great hope is that the children of the world have a chance to read this masterpiece early on and that the rest of us, through it, return to our childlike wonder."

~**Ridgely Goldsborough**, Best-Selling Author, *The Power of You*

"I can say without hesitation that no one knows more about inspiring people to ideate and execute on dreams than Marcia. I regularly incorporate her wisdom and teachings into my legal and business counseling practices with great results and gleefully recommend her to everyone I encounter who wants a dream to come true (which is everyone, including me). Most of all, I admire her deep and passionate desire to support and impassion others. She has made an incredible impact on my life and those whom I touch. Everyone, everywhere, will benefit from the insights and knowledge found within these pages."

~**Steven M. Weinberg**, Award-Winning Business Lawyer and Branding Counselor

"*You cannot find a better coach/mentor than Marcia Wieder. I first heard her speak about dreams from a stage several years ago. As she spoke, the energy in my body started to vibrate at a frequency higher than I had ever experienced. I knew that I must work with her to make my new dreams bigger and realize them faster, and have worked with her privately ever since. She will show you how to clearly define what you really want and how to get it. It's all here in* DREAM. *Read this book and let the words guide you to find your highest purpose and how to accomplish it now!*"

~**Michael Murphy**, Author, *Love Unfiltered* and Founder,
Love from Margot Foundation

"*You know that dream that keeps knocking at the door of your heart and mind? It's not going away. You don't need anyone behind you pushing you to start pursuing it because it is pursuing you. Good news: Marcia is here! Not to push, not to pull, but to walk with you as you say yes to the fuller expression of your life and discover how to realize those dreams. Marcia is a gentle soul with a tenacious character. She is honest and direct, and her no-nonsense guidance comes from doing the work needed in her own life. So take a deep breath, open* DREAM, *open your heart and mind, and discover how to live the life you've imagined.*"

~**Paul R. Scheele**, Ph.D., Co-Founder,
Learning Strategies Corporation

DREAM

DREAM

CLARIFY AND CREATE
WHAT YOU WANT

MARCIA WIEDER

CEO, Dream University®
Founder, The Meaning Institute

NEXT CENTURY
PUBLISHING

DREAM

Clarify and Create What You Want

Published by Next Century Publishing
Las Vegas, Nevada
www.NextCenturyPublishing.com

ISBN: 978-1-68102-062-4
Library of Congress Control Number: 2015913127

Printed in the United States of America

For all who dare to dream—
may you always have the courage to follow your hearts.

CONTENTS

ACKNOWLEDGMENTS

I am blessed to have so many dear friends who love, support, and believe in me and my dreams. You are my core. Patrick Wyzorksi, Tim Kelley, Jodi Gold, Cynthia Kersey, Amy Fox, Marci Shimoff, Arielle Ford, Chris Yelton, Doug Crawford, Michael Gelb, Stephen Dinan, Devaa Haley Mitchell, Ali Maya, Mary Morrissey, Adam Markel, Elizabeth Davidson, Lynn Rose, Kathleen Coady, Lynne Sheridan, Christine Hassler, Michael Silvers, Debbi Dachinger, and too many more to name.

A very special "I couldn't have done it without you" word of appreciation to my team and partners, Ninie Lewis, Doron Libshtein, Carol Rydell, Angela Berg, Ridgely Goldsborough, Hubert Lee, Kelvin Duckett, Michael Ullman, and Rita Ko.

I offer deep gratitude to the amazing folks at Next Century Publishing, to Michael Murphy, and to my editor, Ellen Daly. I salute your conviction to be a new kind of publishing partner for authors and messengers.

I also want to express appreciation to my friends and colleagues in The Meaning Institute and the thousands of Dream Coaches® I've had the privilege to train and certify. You have midwifed me into being a better, more spiritual teacher and I promise to remain a great student. A special thank you to Marianne Williamson and Jean Houston for their support on this book.

Thank you to my family, Murray, Roberta, Audrey and Harvey, Scott and Joy, and the next generation of dreamers—Shira, Carly, Seth, Howard, Randy, and Lindsey. You have been and continue to be my most amazing teachers.

Thank *you* for reading this book and for spreading the word that our dreams are precious and essential. May your life be filled with love, joy, and abundance.

And most importantly, thank you, God, for reminding me that we are all dreamers at heart and for granting me the privilege to do this work. I am humbled and honored to serve.

FOREWORD

Jack Canfield,
Bestselling author of *The Success Principles™* and creator of the
Chicken Soup for the Soul® series

I've been teaching people how to make their dreams come true for more than forty years. During that time, I've had the privilege of helping hundreds of thousands of individuals create the lives they want. But when I reached a point in my life where I needed to take my own dreams to the next level, I knew I needed someone to help me. Without hesitation, I chose to work with Marcia Wieder. As my personal Dream Coach®, she played a key role in helping me navigate a major life transition after I sold the Chicken Soup for the Soul® brand.

We had met just a week earlier at a speaking event. She'd politely detained me as I was trying to escape to the restroom, admitting that she had been trying to talk to me for a long time. She asked if she could have a couple of minutes to tell me why she thought our messages and beliefs were aligned and why we should get to know each other.

"You can if you escort me to the men's room," I told her. So she did. She took me by the arm, and as we walked out of the hotel ballroom, she proceeded to tell me why it would be worthwhile for both of us to have a follow-up conversation about how we might help each other. When I came out of the men's room, she was still there, waiting to escort me back to the ballroom. By the end of that short conversation, I gave her the number to my private line and told her she could call me whenever she liked.

She called me later that week, and after we spent time getting to know a little more about each other, she asked if I'd like to work with her as my personal Dream Coach®. I loved her energy and confidence, and I immediately sensed that she meant business when it came to what I consider the most important business of all: the business of making dreams come true.

"I need to make some big changes in my life," I told her, "so I'm going to say yes!"

We started working together right away with weekly calls. Marcia helped me think bigger about what was possible, clarify what I wanted to accomplish and what I was done with, align myself with those desires, and create a concrete, strategic plan for getting there. One of the key tools she gave me was developing a set of criteria for what to say "yes" to and what to say "no" to in my life. As someone who loves to learn and likes to help as many people as I can, it was time for me to take some time back for myself. We mapped out key areas that were meaningful to me such as family, learning, community, fun, acknowledgment, and prosperity, and then we developed some new systems that helped me say "no," which were life-changing for me.

She has been a good friend and trusted colleague ever since, and I've watched her light up the stage at many of my own events. When she asked me one day why I chose her when I could have worked with anyone, I told her, "Because you're funny, you're feisty, and you hold my feet to the fire."

Marcia knows, as I do, that making dreams come true takes hard work, persistence, and the kind of belief that can withstand repeated rejection and dismissal by others. Back in 1991, I had a dream of changing people's lives through the power of inspirational stories. It troubled me that so many people got their view of the world from the eleven-o'clock news, and it was such a depressing view. I wanted people to see the goodness, love, courage, and compassion that human beings are capable of, not just the violence, war, and corruption.

When I was traveling and speaking to audiences across the country, I would weave inspirational stories into my speeches, and people always came up to me afterward and asked, "That story you told about the puppy, or the Girl Scout, is that in a book anywhere?" And I had to say no—until one day, as I was sitting on a plane, I realized that maybe I should be the one to put those stories in a book! I even came up with a title that gave me goose bumps: *Chicken Soup for the Soul.*

I teamed up with my friend Mark Victor Hansen as a co-author, and we got a literary agent and headed to New York City to shop our dream around to publishers. Everyone said the same things. "*Chicken Soup for the Soul* is a stupid title." "The book's too 'nicey-nicey'—no sex, no violence, no edge." "Nobody buys collections of short stories—anthologies just don't sell." All in all, our book was rejected more than one hundred forty times. Even after we collected twenty thousand signatures from people promising to buy the book, we still couldn't get a deal. But I didn't give up. I believed in that dream and I did not believe in letting other people define my future. Finally, after we'd trudged around to every booth at the American Booksellers Association Convention, a small, struggling publisher agreed to print the book. He said if we were lucky, we might sell twenty thousand copies.

My dream had come one step closer to reality, but I didn't stop there. I didn't just want the book to be published—I wanted it to change people's lives. And to do that, it needed to sell. I told our new publisher I was going to sell a million-and-a-half copies in the first eighteen months. He laughed and said I was crazy. But I still believed in my dream. And more importantly, I created a strategy and took action on my dream every day. Mark and I came up with something we called "the rule of five," which meant that every single day we would do five things to promote the book. We wrote down almost a thousand promotional ideas on sticky notes and stuck them on a wall, and every day we would take down five and do them. Some worked; some didn't. But we were doing something right because the *Chicken Soup for the Soul* series went on to become a publishing phenomenon, with two hundred and fifty titles in forty languages, more than one hundred million copies sold in the U.S., and five hundred million around the world.

Dreams are powerful—much more powerful than what most people call reality. If I'd listened to all those "realistic" publishers who rejected the book, or lowered my expectations, I'd have sucked the power out of my dream and I'd never be sitting where I am today. And more importantly, I'd have deprived the countless readers who have told me that *Chicken Soup* books changed their lives, giving them hope, faith, and inspiration to pursue their own dreams. If you have a dream in your heart, it's your job to ensure that it comes true. No one else can do it for you. But the good news is you're not alone.

In *DREAM*, Marcia Wieder has distilled the deep wisdom and practical strategies that inspired me to work with her as my personal Dream Coach®. She has created a step-by-step formula for turning seemingly impossible dreams into everyday realities.

Marcia understands that the most powerful dreams are those that stem from the discovery of your life purpose. As she shares in this book, if you know what you're here on this earth to do, you gain access to the passion that can fuel you through the tough times. And you will find yourself able to communicate that passion to others in such a way that inspires them to support and empower your dream. What enabled me to persist in the face of repeated rejection? My connection to my life purpose, which is *to inspire and empower people to live their highest vision in a context of love and joy.*

She also understands the critical work of overcoming doubt and fear—learning to ignore not only the voices around you that dismiss and reject your dream but the voices inside you as well. Her wealth of experience has taught her how to recognize every pitfall and distraction that could take you off track, and she's created proven strategies for navigating each one. In these pages, you'll find insight, practical advice, and my favorite part—inspiring, real-life stories of dreamers just like you.

This book can act as a Dream Coach® for you, just as Marcia has been for me and for many other people I know and respect, including Fortune 500 CEOs, entrepreneurs, best-selling authors, and corporate teams. Time and time again I've seen her produce extraordinary results, and I know she can do the same for you if you follow her advice and clarify your dream, believe in your dream, and take action on your dream, every day.

Are you ready? It's time to bring out your most cherished hopes and dreams, and brush off the dust of disappointment, doubt, and past failures. By the time you're done reading *DREAM* and following the steps it lays out, I can assure you they'll be beginning to come true.

Here's to your dream!

Jack Canfield

INTRODUCTION

Dream is a verb. This might be obvious, but it's a key concept to keep in mind if you are to use this book the way I intend. *DREAM* is designed, first and foremost, to help you understand who you are and why you are here, and then to help you *take action* to transform your life and contribute to making the world a better place. Of course, "dream" is also a noun, because we speak about having, pursuing, and achieving our dreams. But more importantly, dream is something you do—or should do.

I've been writing, speaking, and teaching people about how to make dreams come true for more than thirty years. In my travels around the world I meet people who dream and who have dreams, and many who don't. Some think dreaming is too hard; some are afraid they will fail; others believe they're too old or can't afford to dream. Some have forgotten how. Some have never learned how. Some have boxed up their dreams and stored them away deep inside, convinced they're nothing more than impossible fantasies.

A dream without action is guaranteed simply to remain a nice idea or concept, a hope or a daydream. The difference between successful dreamers and daydreamers is that successful dreamers act. That's why I call my work a dream *movement*—because it's all about action. My mission is to redefine dreams so that we move away from doubt or hopelessness about them, or from simply thinking, talking, or daydreaming about them. Please don't give dreaming a bad name by simply, well, dreaming.

We were created to create, and your ability to dream is paramount and fundamental when it comes to living a dream-come-true life. This book is designed to help you take real steps toward the dreams that matter to you most.

Why? Because I know you are serious about making them real or you wouldn't be reading this. You are dreaming (the verb) for the sake of manifesting your dreams (the noun).

Many people ask me why I chose the word "dream." Years ago, when I announced to my family and friends that I was closing my marketing business to become a "dreams-come-true consultant," they thought I was nuts. "Oh Marcia, you used to be so credible. Can't you call this goal-setting? Do you have to use the word dreams?" they asked.

I think goal-setting is important, but there's a different kind of energy released around dreams. Our dreams are spacious and creative. You don't need to know how to make a dream happen. You don't even have to believe it's possible, to begin with, at least. The dreaming process itself gets you to swing outside of "being realistic," and this opens new doors and creates fresh opportunities. There's a reason why, when Martin Luther King, Jr., gave his historic speech, he didn't say, "I have a goal," or "I have a strategic plan." He said, "I have a dream." And so do you.

In *DREAM*, I will show you how to discover your purpose and live *on purpose* because there's nothing that will bring you greater fulfillment. Then we will design a life that is the highest expression of your purpose by creating dreams in every area of your life, personally and professionally.

My company, Dream University®, has been providing inspiring and practical tools and resources for decades, and we are known for helping you bridge your inner and outer worlds. In the inner realms, we explore your purpose, mission, and calling. In the outer, we guide you in bringing these gifts out into the world in a way that can touch, serve, and contribute. In the early days, some would label my company and our content as "soft" because of the focus on inner work. But I know this for certain: Without the inner work, the outer doesn't. We need both. When both the inner and outer are aligned, you can have a greater impact and, if you choose, you can monetize your dreams. Not all dreams are or need to be moneymakers or business opportunities but if you choose to pursue your dream full-time rather than part-time, or as a hobby, monetizing it is useful.

That being said, I didn't write this book simply to show you how to attain more stuff, like houses, cars, or money, although you can certainly use this for that. I wrote *DREAM* to help you remember who you are, value your gifts, and teach you how to dream so we can create a world filled with love, joy, and abundance for all. I invite you to join me in the bigger collective vision where we all contribute to making the world a better place.

You are holding in your hands the definitive work on making your dreams actually come true, having the life you love, and living a life filled with passion. In essence, this book is a toolkit for expanded thinking and a roadmap for creating a meaningful life.

When you've finished reading this book you will know:

- Who you really are

- How you want your life to be

- How to develop dreams that inspire you

- How to look at your life with a fresh perspective

- How to remove fear, doubt, and other obstacles

- How to implement the techniques and shortcuts you learn

Beginning with the first chapter, you will learn to empower yourself and believe in your dreams. Possibilities you never knew existed will emerge, and you will begin to trust the resources in your life to help you produce amazing results with greater ease.

Sound enticing?

The Dream Formula

My approach to making any dream come true follows a simple but powerful formula. At school, you learned your ABCs—at Dream University®, you'll learn your CBAs.

1. **Clarify** Your Dream.

2. **Believe** in Your Dream.

3. **Act** on Your Dream.

All three steps are essential to your success. In Part One of this book, you'll get your dreams out of your head and examine them in detail in order to gain clarity. This step is critical, yet for many it's the hardest one. Since our minds are filled with agendas, lists, and, worst of all, reasons why we don't believe we can have what we want, talking about our dreams and writing them down is the first step toward achieving them. To get in touch with the dreams that are most important to you, we'll take an inner journey to reclaim your Essence and discover your purpose; then we can throw open the doors of possibility and let your imagination run free.

In Part Two, you'll be invited to take an honest look at where you are now, in relationship to your dreams. Too often, people don't believe in their own dreams. They listen to the voice of the Doubter inside, and they shut down the voice of the Dreamer. I'll help you identify these two different parts of yourself, and learn techniques for dealing with your Doubter and committing to your Dreamer. You'll unearth the unconscious beliefs and behaviors that are creating obstacles to the fulfillment of your dreams, and create space for unexpected potential to enter your life.

Finally, in Part Three, you'll get to demonstrate that you really do believe by taking action. Without action, dreams are simply nice ideas. But the good news is that once you are clear about what you want, and choose to believe in yourself and your dreams, strategy is the easiest part. You'll learn how to turn dreams into projects that *project* your desires into the future, how to create a support team, and how to be paid well for doing what you love. Yes, it is possible!

This process can be used on any personal or professional dream. It has helped people double, and even triple their incomes, and I've used it with businesses to launch marketing campaigns. I've also used it to help people find love, change careers or lifestyles, travel the world, and more. (You'll read many of their stories in this book.)

The core of the formula is passion. Passion is what excites and compels you, what makes your life rich and extraordinary. This book will show you how to discover or rediscover what you're passionate about and how to invite it into all areas of your life. Passion—or the lack of it—was the seed that got me started on the journey to writing this book, and it is still the fuel for everything I do.

For ten years I lived in Washington, D.C., and was president of a marketing and creative services agency with as many as fourteen employees. Although successful by many people's standards, I was not passionate about what I was doing, how I was doing it, the people with whom I was doing it, and where I was doing it. One day I asked myself a most confronting question: How do I want my life to be? The reason it was confronting is because as someone who strives to live with integrity (essential to living a dream-come-true life) the next question had to be: And what am I willing to do about it?

I took an inventory of my life and saw that I was seriously unhappy. Unhappy with my business, my body, my bank account, my boyfriend, even the building I lived in. My "B list" added up to an F for failure. I was failing at my own life.

As you will soon see, a simple yet profound question to ask yourself is, "Are you more committed to your dreams or to your reality?" That's the question I had to ask myself. I had dreams. My dream was to be free to travel anywhere, anytime, free to do what I wanted when I wanted. My dream included a magnificent view of water and mountains; clean, fresh air; and a quiet, healthy environment.

My dream had me partnering with creative visionaries to make an impact on the world, in addition to traveling the world in style and elegance, speaking about something inspiring and being paid well for doing what I loved. Plus, I wanted to have fun, create my work as play, and live a life filled with joyful self-expression.

Sound outrageous?

Once I had clarity on my dream, strategy and action were the easy parts. I picked up and moved to California. I became a successful life coach, speaker, and author. Back then, no one knew what a coach was outside of the sports arena (now it's a multi-billion-dollar industry). I trademarked Dream Coach®.

I've worked with thousands of people, personally and professionally. I've helped entrepreneurs who were just getting started, as well as senior leaders and their teams in some of the biggest and most wonderful companies in the world. I help them get clear about their vision and mission, and support them as they get into action on their dreams and lives. I lead Dream University® programs for visionaries and big dreamers. I'm very proud that my body of work is taught in schools, companies, prisons, and shelters. I get paid to travel all over the world, inspiring people to dream. I look and feel ten years younger and I'm the healthiest I've ever been. I'm completely free and very happy.

If all of that sounds too good to be true, let me assure you that this is not a Pollyanna approach nor do I believe you can simply click your heels together to produce results. This is the real world so your ability to both dream and manifest requires focus, action, and work. In every chapter you will find clarity as well as the action steps that will prompt you to take your next step, again and always.

DREAM provides proven methods for achieving everything you want in life. The exercises will help create a personal record of what you learned about your dreams and how to accomplish them. I encourage you to choose a journal or notebook that you can use for these exercises, or create a digital journal—throughout this process, I'll be referring to this as your Dream Book, in which you can look back at and see the progress you are making. You can also go to DreamUniversity.com/DreamBook to download a free specially designed PDF Dream Book.

I'm acutely aware that we live in challenging times, and the media and many people will try to convince you that this is not the time to dream but rather the time to be realistic. I'm going to show you that it's never been a better time and *DREAM* will demonstrate this to you with real world concepts, principles, and stories.

Regardless of how old you are, where you live, or any other circumstances, you can create your reality. Who hasn't had setbacks, losses, and disappointments? Don't let that be justification for giving up on what's important to you.

Just like you, I've had successes and failures, moments I've celebrated, and memories I've had to grieve. When I first set out in pursuit of my dream, as I watched my checking and savings accounts dwindle, my doubts and fears crept in. I was afraid I was going to run out of money, fail, and prove that everyone else was right and my idea was crazy. But somehow I just never gave up. I believed in myself enough to continue to take the next step, and I believed in my dream enough to know it deserved more of my energy and commitment. So I stayed the course. Even though I got scared, confused, and frustrated, I just kept going. And along the way I made so many extraordinary discoveries about what it really takes to make dreams come true and what prevents most people from succeeding. As you'll discover in this book, it's probably not the things you imagine that will be the biggest obstacles.

Everything I teach comes from personal experience. I've been challenged, learned from it, lived through it (always, because I am still here) and have come out the other side with more meaningful dreams than ever. And my biggest dream these days is to be able to use everything I've experienced to help millions of people like you believe in their dreams.

This book is written with you as its focus. You can use it as if it were a highly paid Dream Coach® taking you by the hand to lead you through the process. Interact fully with its pages and, when you are done, I believe you'll say, "Yes, I can make my dreams come true anytime I choose." Reconnect to your passion, find and create dreams that honor your heart's desire, and prepare for the magic and surprises that are available to all dreamers. *DREAM* will teach you exactly how to do this.

Let's get started.

PART ONE

CLARIFY *Your Dream*

CHAPTER 1

Dream Your Dream

All human beings are also dream beings.
Dreaming ties all mankind together.

—Jack Kerouac

I was leading a Dream Retreat in Maui when I received the phone call. *The Oprah Winfrey Show* was looking for a "passion expert." Thrilled and honored, I jubilantly exclaimed, "You want me!"

"We're interviewing thirty authors," the show producer replied, coolly.

A little less enthusiastically, I thought to myself, "You could still want me."

"Tell us why we should select you," she continued. "You have three minutes."

I quickly ran through the highlights of my credentials, including being featured on PBS-TV, being a columnist for the *San Francisco Chronicle*, even starring in an infomercial on passion. I shared accomplishments that I was most proud of such as helping thousands of people find, create, and accomplish their dreams and certifying hundreds of Dream Coaches® to lead my work. I even expressed my mission, "To educate and inspire people and companies to achieve their dreams."

I didn't fail to mention how much I respected Oprah as a visionary who impacts millions of people every day and how I saw us as kindred spirits. I told her all of this in under three minutes while my heart pounded fiercely in my chest.

She thanked me and said, "We'll get back to you."

Sometimes, when it comes to important dreams, all we can do is give it our best shot, hope for the highest good, and let it go. Knowing I could use all the help I could get, I prayed.

Early the next morning, my phone rang. "We picked you!" the producer said.

I shrieked, and then replied (somewhat) calmly, "I really value feedback. Can you please tell me why you selected me as your passion expert?"

"Yes," she said. "It was simple. You were clearly the most passionate."

This made a true believer out of me on a point I often teach. Passion sells! Most of us would rather do business (and more) with people who love what they are doing (and show it) than with someone who is just doing a job.

When Oprah calls, you fly. I was expected to be in Chicago the following Monday. Luckily I had flown to Maui directly from giving a keynote speech so I had a suit with me. Otherwise I would have had to either go shopping or show up wearing a Hawaiian muumuu.

The program was about empowering people to follow their dreams. Having never been on national television, I was, understandably, quite nervous, but also excited. We were one segment into the show when something compelled me to blurt out, "Oprah, what was your dream when you started your company?"

After the show, her team told me, "Oprah usually asks the questions." I was embarrassed but Oprah was so lovely and funny that I quickly got over it. I guess she didn't mind either because I have since been invited back.

Oprah responded, "My dream was to create a great place to have fun." Here was one of the richest and most powerful women in the world and she was telling me she places a high value on having a good time. I can attest to this because before the show, we laughed together in the green room when she confessed, "I found out at an early age that people would pay me to talk and I've been talking ever since."

Looking out at the audience in the studio, Oprah continued, "My big dream was to create a company where people would gather, make a contribution, and together we'd give back to the world." The audience went wild, hooting and hollering, shouting out, "You're doing it, Oprah!" As the energy in the room reached a fever pitch, Oprah calmly turned to me and asked, "What's your dream, Marcia?"

As her microphone suddenly appeared in front of my mouth, I had this thought. Most of us don't like to share our dreams publicly or even one-on-one. Why? If I tell you my dream you might laugh at me or I might fail, and then what you will think of me? But I know for a fact that there's a deeper reason why many of us don't want to share our dreams. Are you ready? It's because if you tell me your dream, I might expect you to do something about it!

Of course, those of us who are serious and committed to achievement know how powerful it is to have others support us in making those dreams a reality. But that doesn't make sharing them any less intimidating.

If it's intimidating to share your dreams one-on-one, picture this. Thirty-five million people (and my mother) watch *Oprah*. I took a deep breath and said, "My dream is that we'll have dreams again." Oprah nodded as I went on, "And that we'll stop thinking of them as unattainable fantasies and take the first or next step toward achieving them."

Oprah smiled at me as we went to a commercial break. Here's a behind-the-scenes story. She came over to me, placed her hands on my shoulders, looked deep into my eyes, and said, "Marcia, you know something that I know."

All I could think was, "I'm having a moment with Oprah." My mind went blank and I couldn't focus on what she was saying. I shook myself out of my stupor as she continued with these powerful words: "It's all about dreams. If I had to attribute my success in life to any one thing it is this: I believed in my dreams, even when no one else did."

No wonder she is where she is today. And I'd like to add this to Oprah's wisdom: Sometimes there is no evidence that your dream is a good idea. I don't like that, but it's a fact. And sometimes there is no evidence that this is the right time to pursue your dream, especially if it's a big one.

But where are you looking for evidence? Don't look in your checkbook or in the stock market or on the evening news for assurance. The only place to look to decide whether or not you believe in your dream is in your own heart. Can you believe in something simply because it matters to you, and can you prove that you truly believe in it by taking action today?

Bringing Dreams Down to Earth

Most people think of dreams either as unattainable fantasies or as something they have in their sleep. Neither of these definitions are what I mean when I speak of dreams.

I define dreams as the aspirations, desires, goals, and hopes that you most want for yourself. Moreover, these are the kind of dreams you have while you are very much awake.

The word "dream" has long been misinterpreted, as if dreams were like puffy clouds in the sky—beautiful, but unreachable. Although "dream" suggests possibility and hope, most people have a sense of hopelessness and futility about their dreams. Yet, their dreams continue to live like embers, flickering in the back of their minds or deep in their hearts.

Using this book, you will learn to create clarity about what you want and get your dreams out of your head and into your life. Life without dreams is no life at all. When our existence gets reduced to a list of problems to solve or things to check off, passion dries up. Without our dreams, all we have is reality. Reality is not a bad thing; in fact, it's essential. We have to know where we are in order to design the strategy for where we want to go. But the question is, what has being overly realistic cost you?

If you're overly realistic it can cost you your passion and joy, your creativity and desire, and take years off your life. Reality is an important part of the mix, but being too realistic can squelch your passion and dreams. Many use the word "realistic" like a pair of handcuffs, keeping them chained to some unexplored limitation.

One person who could never be accused of being overly realistic was a guy named Don. At thirty-eight years old, most people, especially men, might think it unrealistic to begin a career as a professional dancer. But not Don. It was a dream he had for a long time and he felt ready, so he called Ron Guidi, the artistic director for the Oakland Ballet in California. Ron said he loved Don's moxie, and talent and guts usually went hand in hand. He agreed to let Don audition.

Don was great, so Ron told him the reality of his situation. If Don would practice and train six hours a day, six days a week, in six months he could go on stage with the ballet. Ron also told him that realistically, he would have much greater opportunities and success as a dancer in musicals. This thrilled Don and it was the beginning of his professional dance and theatrical career. In this case, their conversation about being realistic created more opportunities than limitations.

Don't let being realistic suppress your dreams—take action on your most audacious hopes and possibilities, and then let reality guide you as you bring them into being. Don's dream may have sounded unrealistic, but what made him different from dreamers who are actually daydreamers or wishful thinkers is that he took action. Most daydreamers never take any substantial action on their dreams. This is how you can spot them. By taking action, Don quickly found a "realistic" way to live his dream.

Even medical professionals agree that people with passion and dreams live longer, healthier lives. My colleague, Dr. Mehmet Oz, shared with me the medical term "apoptosis," otherwise known as "programmed cell death" or "cell suicide." He explained that when your brain believes you have outgrown your usefulness, which can happen at any age, it sends a message to your cells that they are no longer needed and people start to mentally and physically self-destruct. We see this most often when people retire, get laid off, experience an empty nest, or just stop dreaming. Without dreams, we simply don't have a reason to get out of bed. Therefore, not only is dreaming not selfish; it's an act of generosity to have dreams for yourself and the people you love. You will live longer and have a better quality of life than those who are just going through the motions, being "overly realistic," or feel that they are too old to dream. Talking to an elderly person about taking their medication or vitamins to add a few more years to their life is nowhere nearly as effective as inspiring them to imagine dancing at their grandchild's wedding.

I saw an example of this phenomenon all too close to home. My father, Murray, had always been healthy and active, and he'd always been a dreamer. Growing up on the wrong side of the tracks in the Bronx, he didn't have an easy start in life, but when he fell in love with my mother, who was from the right side of the tracks, he didn't let his circumstances get in the way of his dream of dating her. He couldn't afford even to take her to dinner, so he became a very successful pool hustler and used his winnings to date my mother. One of his main marks was a guy called Bernard Schwartz, who would later become famous as Tony Curtis, the movie star.

So my father had never been afraid to dream big or act on his dreams. But last year, he was diagnosed as having lymphoma. Even though the doctor told him it was slow-growing and he would outlive it, somebody planted the seed of a belief in my father's mind that he was dying. That was all it took. He put on a bathrobe and slippers, and my active, youthful father, who previously had a six handicap in golf, was now shuffling around the house. I got the emergency call from my mother: "You'd better come down—your father is dying." So I flew to Florida and was shocked to see him looking and acting like an old man. I saw instantly that he didn't have any dreams, and therefore, had no reason to live. The story he had told himself about his cancer was overshadowing his aliveness and vitality.

"Dad, you need a new dream!" I told him that afternoon, as we walked slowly down his street.

"I'm too old to have new dreams," he retorted.

"Okay," I said. "But what about your lifelong dream—the one you always said you wanted to fulfill before you died?"

He glared at me, but I persisted. "The safari trip to Africa?"

Now I'd gotten his attention. He stopped and looked me in the eye.

"I will make that dream come true," I told him.

"What's the catch?" he asked, as he always did.

"Well," I replied, "there is a catch. One, you have to get physically in shape so we can bounce around for hours in a jeep through the open terrain. Two, I will take you on this trip but you are not allowed to complain. You get one get-out-of-jail-free card, but if you complain after that you're paying for your own trip. If you complain again, you're paying for mine…"

He snorted. "Over my dead body!"

Taking his arm, I told him, "That's what we are trying to avoid."

And he did it. He started walking in the pool, jogging, and getting back into his rhythm and out of his bathrobe. We took that trip to Africa, and I'll never forget the precious moment when we had the privilege of seeing one of the last surviving black rhinos. Dad turned and looked at me with a tear in his eye and gave me a thumbs-up.

When he returned home, he kept up his exercise regime. He chose to live because he had connected to a dream. That was the spark that woke him out of his trance. I believe that having a dream and pursuing it will add ten good years of quality living to my father's life.

Dreams belong in every stage of our lives. The ideal situation, which I'll discuss in detail in chapter thirteen, is bringing more of what you love into your everyday life, including the way you make a living. Most of us will work one hundred thousand hours before we retire. Do you love what you're doing, tolerate it, or really despise it? Life is short. Use your precious days, hours, and moments wisely.

Paul Scott, who was a senior vice president at a large telecommunications company, had a passion for fun and he demonstrated it all day every day at work, even under times of change and pressure. Because one of his true passions was golf, he was always willing to entertain and educate important clients out on a beautiful course. And why not? He totally got the importance of passion, as did his exceptional and cutting-edge company. In fact, they hired me to design and implement a year-long program called "The Passion Plan." They knew that happy people make happy employees, and happy employees produce better results.

You can start making your personal and professional dreams come true today—right now—by being clear about what your dream is, by believing in your dream, and by taking simple steps.

What Is Your Intention?

When I listen to people as they discuss their dreams, they seem so quick to abandon what they want. The response is often something like, "Well, it might be nice, but it will probably never happen, so why bother?" Are you simply dismissing your most heartfelt desires? Do you even know what they are?

In talking to people about what they want, I find that most of them don't believe their dreams will come true unless something miraculous happens: if they win the lottery, if Mr. or Ms. Right rides up on a white horse, or if the stars are aligned in the heavens.

Here is a simple and powerful distinction between a dream and a fantasy. With a dream, like owning your own business or traveling the world, you can design a strategy for making it happen. With a fantasy, like winning the lottery, there is nothing that you can do to make sure it happens. Sure, fantasies can occur, but again, there is nothing you or I can do to ensure it.

Keep in mind that you are the one who needs to make the distinction. When I announced to friends and family that I was moving to California to become a Dream Coach®, they thought it was a fantasy and were concerned about my sanity. But I believed in my dream, I could conceive of the strategy, and I was committed to making it happen. Therefore it was a dream, and one that did come true. Dream University® is now a multimillion-dollar business.

A dream can be exotic or glamorous, but it does not have to be. Your dream can be anything from spending more time with your family to starting or growing a business. It can be to become healthier and more physically fit, or to write a book. It could even be as simple as having a great connection with a friend today, or taking a whole day to pamper yourself. Dreams can range from the mundane to the esoteric, and sometimes what you truly want may come as a complete surprise to you. Dreams come in all sizes. No dream is too big and no dream is too small.

Where do dreams come from? Believe it or not, you make them up! Some arise out of need, others out of desire, others appear mysteriously and you can't even say where they came from. In this book, I'll walk you through a process for getting in touch with the dreams that come from the deepest part of who you are and express the unique purpose you're here to fulfill.

The first step in doing that is to set an intention.

Take a fresh page in your Dream Book and put into a single sentence the essence of what you're committed to achieving, getting, doing, or attaining in your life by the time you finish reading this book. What changes do you want to make? It doesn't matter if you can't define all the details; they'll come as you move forward. If you don't believe it's possible, don't worry—we'll deal with beliefs in chapter eight. If you don't know how to achieve it, don't worry—we'll deal with strategy in chapter eleven. For now, just imagine that time, money, and all your other life circumstances were not an issue. Imagine that you had the support of all the people around you and you knew you could not fail. What intention would you set for yourself then?

The key is to get in touch with what you feel passionate about, what excites and motivates you. And if you don't know what that is, you could simply write, "My intention is to have a dream," (trust me, you are not alone on this one). Or you could start small and write down one simple thing you would like to have or do.

If you can't formulate it yet, make something up. Start someplace. Although it might seem ridiculous now, it will often work to lead you down the right path. Think about a time in your life when you spoke to others about an idea, and your idea turned into something more concrete. Perhaps the more you talked about your concept, the more real it became. Getting your intention out of your head gets the ball rolling.

Here are some examples of intentions my clients started with:

My intention is to know what I want and how to get it.

My intention is to find a new job that is more fulfilling to me.

My intention is to get out of debt.

My intention is to have a more intimate relationship with my family.

My intention is to feel more inner peace.

What Are Your Expectations?

Here's another way to think about your intention: What do you expect to be the result when you've finished reading this book? One of the critical skills for being a dreamer is to have expectations. It seems that over the years, having expectations has somehow gotten a bad rap. We've been told that it's not good to expect too much and many of us have been trained to believe that expectations lead to disappointment. Although this well-intended message might have been designed to protect us, it has become the foundation for some of our biggest limiting beliefs as well as tremendous amounts of fear. So as you embark on the journey of this book, I'd like to encourage you to have expectations—even big ones.

Perhaps you're looking for a blueprint to get you from where you are to where you want to be. Maybe you're seeking a strategy or steps that will divide the work of reaching your dreams into defined areas of concentration. Most importantly, I hope you have a specific dream that you expect to come true by the time you finish reading this book.

You can turn this book into an action plan by deciding now what you expect to have happen by the time you've finished reading it. My goal is that you fulfill your dreams as you complete the book; if that's not also your goal, you may want to put the book down now, and think about why you bought it in the first place.

That first step may be enough for you right now. Perhaps you will decide that you just want to be in greater action toward your dream, or that you want your dream to come true in its entirety by the end of this book. It's all up to you. Have a sense of humor and play with it; it doesn't need to be hard work. Enjoy the process.

You probably have more than one dream, even if you don't see them all right now. I'll be encouraging you to open your mind to all kinds of dreams and explore how you want your life to be, and in chapter four, I'll guide you through some "dreamstorming" exercises to open up the possibilities in your future. However, I will be recommending that as you work through this book, you start with one dream, complete the process, and then you can go back and use the same techniques to make your dreams come true in the other areas of your life. To have an experience of the entire process from beginning to end, I do recommend, at least for the first pass, taking yourself through the process on one specific dream. This will help you to get clarity on what you do and don't want, identify and overcome doubts and any other limiting beliefs, and, most importantly, move into action.

Ultimately, you will be able to work on multiple dreams. As a matter of fact, I will be teaching you a shortcut process in which you will see that as all of your dreams are aligned with your purpose, you can check off one and make progress on many simultaneously. That's a wonderful thing. But before you start jumping around or get scattered, since my main intention is to help you clarify what you want, following the process through completely on a specific dream that really matters to you is the ideal way to approach this process.

The techniques await you. Don't sit back to see how it unfolds; it *won't* happen unless you interact with the process. Let this book make a difference in your life; use it to pull you forward so you can get what you want. Start now.

The Impossible Dream

I was speaking at a church near Portland, Oregon, when I met Wilson. A tall, bright-eyed eighteen-year-old, he confided in me that he was a Masai warrior from Kenya, Africa, and this was his first time away from his tribe. I asked what he was doing in Oregon and he told me this tale:

"When I was young, I became ill and my mother took me to a medical clinic. From that day forward, my dream was to become a doctor. But it was impossible since there was no training available and no one ever left the tribe. It just wasn't done.

"As I grew up, I shared my dream with anyone who would listen. Everyone, including my own family, told me it was a fantasy and to forget about it. But I never did. Recently, a writer came from your country to visit my tribe. He interviewed me and published my story. Perhaps you know the paper, *The Washington Post?*"

I smiled and nodded.

He continued, "A couple from Portland read my story and within a matter of weeks I was invited to apply for undergraduate work at the University of Portland. A few months later, I was accepted."

I took a deep breath and said, "That's extraordinary. You must have been so happy."

His response startled me. "Actually, it was one of the most painful days of my life. My family didn't have the money or any other resources to send me off to America on what they considered to be a whim. I knew there was only one thing to do. I prayed for a miracle. And Marcia," he paused, "that's what I got. Four families each came forward to generously extend their hearts and hands. Each agreed to house me, to feed me, to buy my books, and to be my family while I was so far from home."

I swallowed hard as my eyes welled up. But what he said next rocked my world.

"After hearing you speak so passionately about dreams, I now know what I must do. I must become a doctor, of course; that is my dream. But then I must return to my village as an example that no dream is impossible and that extraordinary things can happen when we gather together as a tribe."

Wilson's moving story illustrates something I discovered early in my work as a Dream Coach®. I used to believe that anything was possible as long as I could figure out in advance how to do it. Eventually I realized this was a limiting belief because sometimes the perfect strategy might not be immediately evident. I was stopping myself from going for what I wanted, often before I even began. Just because you don't have a viable plan all mapped out doesn't mean you can't believe in your dream. If Wilson had let not having a plan stop him, he might never have told the reporter from the *Washington Post* about his dream.

Now I believe that *everything is possible.* Believing in our dreams is often what gives us the courage to act on them, to take the important steps forward. In Part Two of this book, we'll focus more on what it means to believe in your dreams and what can get in the way of that belief. But as you begin the process of clarifying and defining your dreams, remember not to limit yourself by letting yourself or other people dismiss your dream as a fantasy. Your dreams are as real as you dare to make them.

CHAPTER 2
Reclaim Your Essence

Intimacy is being seen and known as the person you truly are.

—Amy Bloom, Author of *Lucky Us*

In order to dream, you need to know what you want, which comes from knowing who you are. Each one of us has a story about who we are, and that story shapes the way we see the world. Everything you think and know, or think that you know, is based on your worldview, which comes from your story about who you are. And here's the critical point: your story is only part of the truth. In order to deepen your dreams and get in touch with your passion, it's time for more to be revealed about who you are.

We all share the same basic human needs: We want to know that we matter, that we are loved, and that we belong. We need to be valued and find self-acceptance and appreciation for who we are and the lives we are living. To reveal yourself to yourself requires the fortitude for deep, honest exploration and it is often a challenging inner journey. I can share prescriptions for navigating some issues, but the bottom line, which may be no surprise, is that without you doing the "inner work," there's no real transformation. If you're feeling impatient to get practical in creating your dreams, or if you think this kind of talk is too "woo-woo" for you, I'd encourage you to put those feelings and thoughts aside and trust the process. Believe me, this inner work is essential for the outer work to have power.

Your story—what you believe and how you continually recount it to yourself and to others—can be liberating or limiting. In this chapter, you'll have an opportunity to see it through a new lens and explore a new ending for a tale that is still unfolding. When you can see and understand that your story is still being written, your relationship to it and your life can shift. When you begin to understand that your life is not fixed based on something that did or did not happen to you or for you, you can rewire your circuitry.

Before we take a deep dive into your inner world, let me introduce a few terms I'll be using in this chapter, which refer to different aspects of who you are. First, I'll be talking about *Essence*. By Essence, I mean the fundamental nature of who you are, who I am, who we each are, at the very core. It's the pure consciousness that you were before your life story unfolded. Before we incarnated into a body, all of us were whole and perfect. Your essential self and my essential self came from the same Source.

There's another important term—Source. To some extent, what it means is indefinable, because it points to the mystery of where we all came from and why we are here. You don't have to have any particular beliefs about these matters to benefit from the practices and principles in this book. Your interpretation of Source might just be "all that is unknown and unseen," or "something bigger than my personal world." If you have particular religious or spiritual beliefs, you may like to use the term God, Higher Power, Love, or Higher Consciousness. However, if those terms make you uncomfortable, choose something that feels right for you. This system for making dreams come true does not rely on any particular ideology.

I may occasionally use the term *soul*, which for some people has religious connotations. However, I simply use it to refer to the deep, rich, magnificent part of you that is in touch with your Essence and knows you are a perfect and exquisite expression of love masquerading as a human being.

Lastly, there's the term *ego*. This can be a confusing term, so it's important to define clearly what I mean when I use that term. Ego can be understood as the conscious mind, the sense of "I" that unifies our sensations, thoughts, feelings, and perceptions into a coherent persona that is clearly differentiated as a unique individual. Some people, particularly some spiritual teachers, tend to frame the ego as "bad" or negative. That is not my approach at all. As you'll see as this chapter unfolds, the ego plays a critical function in your life, and it is something to be grateful for. However, you'll also learn how to ensure that the ego is in service to the soul, and not the other way around.

Your Sacred Wound

I am not a therapist, but as both a student and teacher of many philosophies, personal growth techniques, and ancient traditions, I have a perspective informed by my own experience. My intention is not to analyze but rather to offer tools for you to see who you have become and are still becoming—tools that can provide overview, insight, and an appreciation of your life, especially the challenges that you've navigated through, and allow you to open to bigger, deeper dreams. When it comes to the work of understanding ourselves, there is one theory and practice that I have found to be particularly powerful. It comes from the wise teacher Jean Houston, and I am grateful to her for allowing me to share it in these pages.

Over the ten years that I've been teaching this particular theory, I remain in awe at both its simplicity and the depth of insight it provides. Many have reported that it has brought true understanding to their life. One client told me that while working with this practice, he found in fifteen minutes the answer to something he had struggled with for decades in therapy. It is called the *sacred wound*. I'll explain the basic theory before guiding you in an exercise to identify your own sacred wound and sharing some stories to show where it can lead you.

You were born whole and complete, as Essence, as your essential self. However, like every human, at a young age you were wounded. This doesn't mean you were broken. It just means that difficult events happened. They happen to all of us. Sometimes these events can be minor. For example, as a baby you may have cried and no one came to tend to you. Sometimes they can be huge, traumatic incidents, like the loss of a loved one, some form of abuse, or a terrible accident.

When we are hurt, we learn to defend ourselves. When you were wounded, an internal protector, designed specifically to care for the wounded child, came forth. This protector is a function of your ego, and it is well intentioned. But somewhere along the way, your protector became your personality/identity and created a worldview, and began to think it was almighty. The crucial point here is that your identity and worldview were formed by a set of circumstances, interpreted and turned into a story by a child—a story that you still believe. Your life was designed to protect a child. And it formed you into the capable and amazing person you have become.

Of course, we need to protect ourselves from painful or dangerous situations, but here's the challenge: To be defended against anything is to be defended against everything. With our defenses up it's hard for anyone to see us, and it can also be difficult for us to feel the beauty of life. Put your hands up in front of you as though you are deflecting a ball coming toward your face. How much can you feel or experience from this perspective? How available for life, or love, are you? You are either open or closed and the ability to create and live a meaningful life and achieve your dreams requires that you be available and receptive.

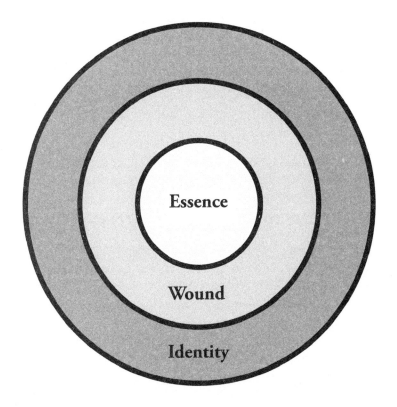

At some point, usually at mid-life, which is more of a mindset than an age, you start to wake up. You begin to ask profound questions, such as, "Who am I? Why am I really here? What is the purpose of my life? What is going to make me truly happy?" Like Rip van Winkle, you awaken from a long slumber of unconsciousness, sometimes even of victimhood and blaming. You realize your story is simply a story and by fully accepting it, while becoming less identified with it, you can put it into perspective.

Back in the seventies, there was a famous commercial for a wine company featuring Orson Welles, with the slogan "No wine before its time." The same is true for your life's journey. You can't force yourself to emerge from behind the defenses of the ego until you are ready. We spend the first half of our life protecting the wounded child and the second half living as the expression of our purpose. And then life gets really interesting and engaging.

Your greatest source of power comes in your second half of life. Once you have your life in order, which includes having your head on straight and your heart open (sometimes after having it broken a few times) your greatest gifts can now be fully revealed and utilized.

And, as a mature adult, you can consciously begin your journey back to Essence. You can use your story and understanding of your personality to consciously revisit your wound, to reclaim lost parts of Essence, as well as the disowned "shadow" parts of yourself, returning to wholeness. This makes you more trustworthy to yourself and others and opens many amazing doors.

Shadow refers to the parts of ourselves that we have hidden, repressed, or denied so they become unconscious. Usually, these shadow parts of ourselves are connected to the original wound. They're the things we vow to "never again" think or feel.

Shadow can also be created by wounds that occur later in our lives, particularly those we feel we cannot bear, or that remind us of earlier pain. Recently, someone I love suffered a terrible heartbreak. On the day she was about to put down a deposit on her wedding dress and venue, her fiancé came home and told her he couldn't marry her. When she told me what had happened, I encouraged her to do two things. First, to feel as much pain as she could tolerate because the appropriate response to loss is grief. When we don't grieve or we deny a loss we cut off from ourselves. Secondly, I urged her not to make any contracts with the universe that started with the words "never again will I..." In the face of pain, despair, or disappointment, we often make extreme and inappropriate vows to ourselves and others, such as, "Never again will I love," or "Never again will I take a risk to trust another with my heart."

With those few little words we close, lock, and bolt doors to new opportunity. When she recently fell in love again, she told me she was deeply grateful for both pieces of advice. The first one helped her move through it and heal more quickly. The second one kept her heart open for love.

Some people worry about seeing or revealing their shadow, concerned about how they will act or what others might think. The irony is that although these parts have been hidden from us, everyone else can easily see them. But we only see them in our dreams, our emotions, and sometimes most commonly, through our reactions to other people.

Awakening and transformation is about making all parts of ourselves known to ourselves. You will soon, perhaps immediately, feel energy and potency as you open locked doors that you didn't have the capacity to deal with as a child. Then everything changes. With your soul no longer commandeered by your ego, your ego can take its proper place in service to your soul. Now you can know and trust your dreams. You can use your identity to be of service, to make a contribution to the world and, to fulfill your highest purpose and destiny.

Here's a thought-provoking idea: What if your life was predestined—your wound, your story, your self-protection, and your journey of awakening and returning to Essence? By whom? God, Source, life, creation? Whichever term you choose, here's the important question to consider: What if you got exactly the wound you needed in order to become the person you have become, to fulfill the destiny you are called to create? I don't mean to suggest that you deserve to have been abused or hurt; I am simply suggesting that you can change your perspective on those events and discover their unique gifts. That's why Jean Houston calls it the sacred wound. When you stop using your wound to justify, blame, criticize, or hurt yourself and others, and rather appreciate the character you have become, your life will completely change. This could happen today. It's true. Transformation can occur in an instant with an insight, choice, or decision. Then you get to spend the rest of the day, or the rest of your life, practicing getting it right and integrating it.

You inherited the life you were given because you were the perfect steward for great insight and wisdom. We've each been to our own version of hell, lived to tell about it, transmuted it into love, and therefore we must be here to teach about it, write about it, speak about it, or simply to share about it. You are here to fulfill a noble purpose and were wounded in exactly the way life needed you to be.

However, if you continue to cling to your old story, it can't morph into the new one that is birthing through you right now. If you hold tight, bracing for impact or terrified to let it go, it will get tired and so will you. If you feel stuck, stifled, bored, uninspired, irritated, or maybe even angry, frustrated, or resentful, consider this: You are the creator of your life and the designer of your destiny. You get to write the second act and include everything you imagine will make you happy and fulfilled.

So, what are you going to do with your second act? How are you going to use your God-given gifts and talents? Your Essence informs your purpose, which aligns with your vision and dreams. To access your Essence and bypass your ego's defenses, you need to uncover your sacred wound. Without knowing who you are and why you're here, you're missing a critical piece of the code.

The following exercise will help you understand your story so you can discover your purpose and create a meaningful life. As you reveal your wound, the questions you need to ask are: What did you make it mean and what did you do with it? What judgments did you pass? What conclusions did you draw?

When we let go of judgments about our lives, we can become insightful witnesses who can share our life lessons with others.

Finding Your Sacred Wound

As a pioneering creator of transformative programs, Dr. Jean Houston explores the nature of spiritual yearning and demonstrates how to facilitate a personal quest for fulfillment. This exercise is one that she created in her book *The Search for the Beloved: Journeys in Mythology and Sacred Psychology*, and is used here with her permission.

The purpose of this exercise is to become less identified with your story so ultimately you can integrate it into your being as opposed to being unconsciously run by it or living as a victim of it. The tricky part is first we have to turn toward a core issue that can be scary or painful for some. But we aren't going to stay there.

Review silently the "woundings" in your life and choose an important one but don't worry about choosing the "right" one. Whatever bubbles up right now is perfect. Either with a partner or in your Dream Book, answer the questions below. Use them to connect to the memory, to recall it and most importantly to feel it. Accessing specific memories and the willingness to feel them is the path to healing.

1. What happened? How were you wounded?

2. What did you feel when you were wounded?

3. What were the full consequences of this wounding in your life, for good or ill?

4. In the light of this, what do you want?

5. What does all this mean? What pattern is playing itself out here?

You get extra points and insight if you do this next part as well. Building upon the answers from the above questions, Dr. Houston suggests that you "'re-remember' [your story] as a myth, assuming the role of myth-maker and telling it in the third person, not as 'I' but as 'she' or 'he' or 'it.'"[1] When creating a myth of your life, you must keep yourself well away from the mundane—something of a trick to do. Dr. Houston provides insight into the approach: "Each figure and situation in the myth is archetypal. Thus a soldier becomes the Warrior, a young girl is the Maiden-to-be-Rescued, an animal may be the Ally, and a serpent the Guardian of the Gates. The child is always Holy, if unrecognized, the circumstances of birth extraordinary; the family always poor but honest, or of the highest nobility (there is no bourgeoisie in the land of myth); an elderly person is the Wise One; the one who yearns is the Lover, the one who seeks, the Hero or Heroine."[2]

Start with "Once upon a time..." and take the story past the wounding to the place of transformation, which is important. Too often we limit ourselves, even in our own imaginations, by saying something like, "Well, I can't say that because it's just not realistic; I could never be that brave (smart, rich, etc.)." This is a myth; it's not supposed to be "the truth"! So, in other words, don't forget to let yourself live "happily ever after."

The ability to creatively tell your story impersonally as a myth can help you begin to be less attached to it as "yours." But let me reiterate an important point. Your story contributed to you being you. It's not the whole story, but nonetheless it did happen. How you see, interpret, and tell it now can change because you'll be less identified with it as being "the only story" or "the whole story." The purpose of this is not to deny or repress it but rather to value it as the gift it has and will continue to be to you. Without your wound, you simply would not be uniquely you.

I'd like to make a distinction here that can be useful. The reclaiming of shadow is what I'd call "consciousness work," and it's quite different than "personal growth" work. Personal growth work is typically about identifying what doesn't work for or about you, fixing it, or even doing away with it. Consciousness work is about seeing, honoring, and accepting all parts of yourself. It may feel counterintuitive to value or appreciate some part of yourself that you judge or even loathe, but it is a transformational path to healing and ultimately great peace.

Your Wound at Work

A client named Pat came to my home for a private one-day work-shop. Pat was an extremely successful realtor but his dream was to be a world-class professional speaker. The problem was, he didn't know what he wanted to speak about. He was, he told me, "confused and frustrated after months of trying to refine my message." I told him to choose a topic about which he was passionate—something that was meaningful to him and that others would value, so they would pay him for it. I explained that it's not enough to be a good speaker. Messengers have real messages and great speakers have something valuable to say. They know who they are, why they are here, and they have a vital message. "If becoming a speaker is your dream," I challenged him, "your ability to reveal who you are begins by doing the depth work required to find your own authentic voice."

I love these private sessions; in just eight hours, I was able to take him to the core of his soul using specific, proven methodologies—like the one I'm sharing in this chapter. To find his message, I invited Pat to write out ten things that he knew, thought, or believed were meaningful to him. It was a useful exercise, mostly for what it revealed. Although his insights were true, they sounded like everyone else in the self-help field. Personally, I am jaded about jargon so with my clients we seek to create a unique brand and message that reflects the one-of-a-kind person each of us is. I knew we had to go deeper.

I asked Pat to tell me how he had been wounded as a child. He had no idea what I was talking about. I asked him to share with me a few painful or difficult memories, assuring him I would hold them in confidence (he later gave me permission to share them here). I did my best to create a safe space for him to let down his guard and his story/persona/identity as a powerful, successful businessman.

Pat told me that as a kid, he had all kinds of dreams and far-fetched ideas. He shared how he found a small, old copy machine and turned that into his first business, serving local merchants who needed copies made, which he delivered in his red wagon. He was excited about all kinds of opportunities but his father did not share his enthusiasm. Pat was scolded and told to get his head out of the clouds and get serious. His father's verbal abuse shut him down and it wasn't long until his grades dropped and he began failing in school. He was ridiculed and further wounded.

I asked him if he had had any wild ideas—similar in quality to his copy delivery service when he was a kid—since he'd been in the business world as an adult. He laughed and said there were many. The most recent one involved renting beer kegs and party materials to his clients so they could throw great bashes. Everyone thought he was nuts, he said, until it made the company over a million dollars.

At that moment, I knew what his brand would be and the unique message that he needed to share. We got on my computer and with just a few clicks, he trademarked CrazyBrilliant. Of course it was available; it was waiting for him and this moment. It was time and it was perfect. Most importantly, he loved it.

Reflecting on what we achieved that day, he said, "In just a couple of hours, a seven-figure business was born! By the end of the day, my entire business model was complete and I left with a concrete plan—feeling confident and prepared to execute." Now Pat speaks about a meaningful message that completely resonates with who he is and why he is on this planet. His wound made him the ideal spokesperson for innovation and creativity. He plans on interviewing people like Tony Hsieh, CEO of Zappos, because we all know selling shoes online is crazy—CrazyBrilliant! He's going to give out CrazyBrilliant awards to people who are taking risks, thinking way outside the box, and aren't stopped by other people's judgments or opinions. He told me the first award was going to my company, Dream University®. When I started my company, people thought I had lost my mind and would starve. They could not have been more wrong.

Not only did Pat design a message that is aligned with who he is and what he believes, but we discovered how to take his wound—a source of pain and shame—and own it, as well as use it for healing others. It doesn't get much better than that.

Pat said his whole life made sense now as he discovered a deep appreciation for his unique way of thinking, which also healed the critic within him. Our parental voices often become our own internal critics as we either do the opposite of what they taught us to spite them or adopt their voices as our own.

Like Pat, you too were wounded in a specific way that enables you to bring a specific gift to the world—a gift that can be used for your own healing and that of others. Discover your wound and as you embrace it from a centered and compassionate place, you won't discover a source of pain but rather a great source of inspiration.

My Wound

Another reason I love the sacred wound work is that it has proven to be transformational in my own life. Here's how understanding my own story of wounding revealed my purpose to me.

The year I was born, my five-year-old sister went deaf. At first my parents thought she was "jealous of the new baby" and perhaps that's why she wasn't listening or doing as she was told. Now, over sixty years old, her handicap has worsened, also leaving her legally blind.

A few things happened to me from this early childhood "story." My father, angry and resentful, banished faith from our home. Isn't it ironic that I grew up to become the "Dream Queen," someone who wants people to be happy, believe in themselves, and have what they want? I became a professional speaker but it wasn't until more than a decade into my career, as audiences increased from hundreds to thousands, and after many national television appearances, that I realized my work was becoming unfulfilling. After taking myself through the same process I offer in this book, I realized that the person I most wanted to be able to hear and see me on stage or TV would never be able to. That was my sister.

In full disclosure, I had spent the first part of my life committed to my story and angry at her, blaming her for robbing me of my childhood, taking away my family, and bringing us such sadness. Unknowingly, I declared to myself that "never again" would I be a victim like my sister. That became my shadow. It was only years later, when I found myself in the midst of a crisis, misunderstood, attacked and persecuted for something I didn't do, that I fell into victim consciousness, a place I realized I'd always avoided. It was at that moment that my own shadow was revealed to me—the hidden agreement I'd had with myself since I was a little girl.

When I saw this, I decided to fly to Florida and sit with my sister. Now in her sixties, she is blind, deaf, and quite severely handicapped, but she has lived a full life and is married with two wonderful sons.

In sitting with her, I felt how helpless I was even to communicate with her, and how helpless she was in the face of her disabilities. All I could do was be with her, help her eat, and help her get around. Overwhelmed by helplessness and hopelessness, I went back to my hotel, exhausted.

And then I realized that my story about her—about how helpless and hopeless she was—was completely wrong. In fact, she was incredibly strong. I felt admiration and appreciation for how she is able to live her life. I was the one who was helpless in that moment, not she. I, who had built my whole identity around hope and being able to do whatever I can dream. And in allowing myself to feel that helplessness, I found the gift, the pearl within my sacred wound: a new level of empathy that I hadn't even realized I was missing. As long as I was holding the victim at arm's length and saying, "I'll never be that," there was a whole world of emotion, feeling, and sensitivity from which I was cut off.

Through becoming conscious of my wound and the meaning I gave it, and embracing my shadow, it shifted from a terrible pain to something I now deeply value. It made me a better sister, friend, coach, and teacher. It gave me access to greater compassion and forgiveness, which ultimately both softened my heart while toughening my skin, so I didn't take things so personally. I began to see myself and the world through new eyes, finding more beauty, gratitude, and appreciation.

The things we're most afraid of are often those that have the greatest power. That sacred wound was the most significant event of my life. My biggest problem and enemy became my greatest ally and gift. I have deep appreciation for it, as well as for the wisdom and rewards it provides. And above all, I have a profound appreciation for my sister, whom I now consider my greatest teacher.

Directly facing your sacred wound produces a sacred life in service to a sacred mission—creating a better world. No one has lived the life you have lived and your unique thumbprint is needed. It's profound to realize that your life, exactly the way that it is, filled with its foibles, failures, and frustrations as well as the miracles and extraordinary moments, is a masterpiece. Now, it's all about what you do with it. Fulfillment comes from discovering who you are and then translating that into a powerful purpose that you can pursue in the world. Now, you're ready to discover yours.

You have been seeded to do great things, whether large or small, and authenticity comes from living in integrity with your heart and soul. It comes from trusting life—specifically, the one you have been given. If you feel called to write a book, speak, or create, and you're afraid it's already been said and done, let me set you straight. No one will deliver the message you're here to deliver because no one has had your life or story and, therefore, your specific point of view. At a certain level, there is no competition, because you are a one of a kind, unique creative expression of life. And without you—your gifts, your insight, your story, and your wounding—life would be incomplete.

CHAPTER 3
Remember Your Purpose

The purpose of life is to live a life of purpose.

—Robert Byrne

"I want to double my business within the next calendar year without burning myself out."

This was the dream my client Larry wrote down during our first session. His goal was reasonable; in fact, it's done all the time. But Larry came to me because he didn't know how to accomplish it and he felt that something was in his way. He just couldn't quite put his finger on what it was.

I told Larry that we'd start the process of making his dream real by getting in touch with what he's passionate about. Larry balked. "Wait a minute," he said. "I don't want to examine my whole life; I just want to know how to double my business."

"Larry, you have to trust the process," I told him. "Passion is everything. Do you know why? Because passion is your access to power."

Larry bravely allowed me to guide him, and he quickly made an important discovery. I asked him to think about what most excited him—what activities lit him up and gave him energy. His answer: having powerful partnerships and intimate relationships.

When he realized the passion he felt about creating partnerships, Larry understood that he needed to learn how to develop associations with anyone at any time, and that this would be the secret to his success.

As we continued to probe, Larry became aware that by holding onto old beliefs that no longer served his needs, he was limiting his potential to create partnerships. For example, he had developed the habit of not "revealing his cards." He feared taking the "wrong" kind of people into his confidence. He worried that others wouldn't uphold their end of a bargain or that they didn't have the "best" credentials to be his partner. He had been eliminating wonderful potential partners before ever giving them a chance. Together, we removed the obstacles, the limiting beliefs that were in Larry's way (we'll talk more about how to do this in Part Two). This had a huge impact and immediately freed him up to dream big.

Once clear about what made him feel passionate, and with his limiting beliefs out of the way, Larry made a conscious commitment to develop partnerships with anyone that he chose. Now he's excited about living his life, not just about doubling his business. He has more than two dozen strategic partnerships with associates, friends, agents, even competitors, all of whom are helping him achieve his dream. Larry understands that passion is a key component in the formula for success and that people are a central part of his passion.

If passion is the access to power, the way to access passion is through your life's purpose. Your purpose is who you are, what gets you excited; I might even say that your purpose is remembering why you're here. I use the word "remembering" because it's not something you have to invent or discover for the first time—it already exists within you, and when you come upon it, you might find yourself saying, "Of course!"

If you're like a lot of readers, you might say, "I picked up this book because I wanted to make my dreams come true, but between you and me, I don't think I have a purpose."

Yes, you do. Your purpose is not a big, burdensome, heavy weight that you must accomplish in your life; rather, it's an expression of who you are. We are each here to learn, grow, and express ourselves. And we each have great gifts and contributions to make as well. Larry didn't increase sales until he defined who he was and realized that his purpose was to create powerful partnerships. After that, it was easy.

Without knowing their purpose, many people climb to the top of the mountain, only to discover it is the wrong mountain. The way to avoid this is to know who you really are by discovering your purpose.

If you are wondering where to find your purpose, you don't need to look far. It resides inside of you. Consider this: an acorn is designed to become a mighty oak tree just as you are designed to grow into the best possible you. What were you uniquely seeded for? We all have particular gifts and talents and are here to leave our mark to make the world a better, more beautiful place.

To live on purpose requires the following three things:

1. Have a spiritual practice so you can hear the deeper wisdom beyond your ego.

2. Know what is unique about you, formed by all of your life experiences, including that which you would celebrate and that which you would grieve.

3. Be of service with your gifts.

Your purpose could be anything that gets your juices flowing; it comes from what turns you on in life. The broader you state it, the better, because the broader your purpose, the more room there is for passion and possibility. If you're concerned that your purpose is not going to be worthy, big enough, or decent enough, here are some examples that others have offered when asked to complete the sentence, "My life's purpose is . . ."

> . . . to live life as an adventure.

> . . . to create joy.

> . . . to be of service.

> . . . to make a difference.

> . . . to go beyond.

> . . . to play and have fun (yes, even this is a noble and worthy purpose).

Your purpose is anything that touches your heart and makes a difference to you. If you're working at a job just for the money, and what you're doing doesn't make you feel proud, perhaps you've lost your sense of purpose. The test is how you feel: Are you turned on or are you so busy reacting to the needs of daily life that you're happy just to be getting through the day?

Most of us spend our lives reacting and responding to clocks and calendars, paying bills and putting out fires. It's hard to live "on purpose" when life revolves around daily crises and you're always feeling overwhelmed. By taking the time to define your purpose, you'll open up more time and space, have more energy, and be more focused. Then your life can change for the better.

A Meaningful Life

I've been studying and teaching about meaning and I know that living a meaningful life with a purpose is an essential dream. As a matter of fact, over the last decades, it's the dream I have heard more than any other. "I want to know that my life has meaning and that it matters," is something I hear regularly in my world travels.

I just spent a week with twenty of the smartest, highest-paid consultants in the world, leading them through my curriculum. Some admitted they had never attended a spiritual workshop (that's what it was labeled since it was not tied directly to business). Upon completion, they rated the program seven out of seven. I believe it wasn't because of the information but because I took them to a place they had never been—I took them to their souls. They saw that success without meaning is empty and will yield limited results. I know, as many of them now realize, that their lives and the lives of the countless people and organizations they impact will be forever altered if they can bring more meaning into their work.

Does your life have meaning? Sadly, for most people the answer is either "not enough" or a flat out "no." There is a deep gnawing or longing in people's souls for more—not for more stuff, but for more meaning. And it turns out that meaning is critically important to performance, well-being, and success. Conversely, a lack of it undermines our ability to function on many levels, including our job performance, mental well-being, and physical health. Studies show that people who report that they are missing a sense of meaning in their lives are more likely to exhibit the chronic stress response associated with life-threatening diseases like heart disease and some cancers.

Two of the critical factors that bring meaning to life are belonging and contributing. But that doesn't mean we don't also need to take care of ourselves. Until you know you can manifest your own needs and dreams, it's often hard to trust that you could do it for and with others. The converse is true. Once I show you how to find your purpose and live on purpose, you are going to have more energy and resources so you will have extra to contribute and serve. Once you taste the sweet success of manifesting what you want, you will have greater confidence to use your skills to help others. And more begets more. Your life will become an example, encouraging others to get clear about what they do and don't want, and contribute to the creation of it.

Then you can focus on the bigger dreams. Yes, a world that is filled with love, joy, and peace for all. We can and must contribute to creating a world that is whole and works for everyone.

Many people in this day and age hold a belief that they are not enough or feel inadequate. Consider this metaphor: if there's a hole in the bucket (or in this case your heart), no matter what you put in—no matter how much money, success, even love—it will always leak out. A million dollars times zero still equals zero. With a hole in the bucket, the richest person might feel poor, and the most popular might feel alone. So we must mend this hole.

The way to do this is to know that you have a specific reason to be here, a destiny to fulfill. You are valuable, even priceless, your life is meaningful, and what you say, think, and do truly does matter.

As you uncover your purpose, you will come to know (or recall) that who you are is exquisite, perfect in every way (flaws and all), and you aren't just okay or adequate, but truly precious and priceless. You are a one-of-a-kind creation!

5 Ways to Discover Your Purpose

You may be wondering how to determine your purpose. Don't worry, you don't have to do it all at once, and certainly not for all time. Life ebbs and flows, and your purpose may modify accordingly over time. In this chapter, I'll share five techniques for discovering (or remembering) your purpose.

1. Look in Your Past

One place to look for what turns you on is to see what has turned you on in the past. Your passionate memories may be of graduating from college, meeting a spouse, or getting a big raise. They may include a special trip you took, a speech you gave, having a baby, running a marathon, or accomplishing an important goal. If you can't find at least three memories of passion—and I promise you've had at least thirty-three, maybe three hundred and thirty-three—you're being too hard on yourself and setting your sights too high. Memorable moments come in all sizes.

It doesn't even matter if you harbor negative reactions about them because anger and frustration can be mighty motivators. When you look back now, were you excited? Did you feel good? If you answer yes to those questions, then write the memory down.

On a fresh page in your Dream Book, list three times in your life from the day you were born to this moment when you felt excited and passionate. Look for three special moments about which you can say, "I did that; it felt good." Write them down simply and quickly; as you write the first one, the other two will come.

When you have three, take a deep breath and relax; the hard part is over. Now look for the pattern, the common theme about those memories. What was present for you in all three examples? What were you passionate about?

If you think at first that there's nothing consistent about the listed events, bring your mind back to the time and place of each situation. Get in touch with what you were feeling then, about the events and about yourself. Avoid narrowing things down; try to stay with broad qualities. Perhaps all the items listed were fun. Maybe they all had a partnership component, or they all made you feel uneasy at first, but you took a risk and did them anyway. Perhaps the accomplishments all went beyond what you thought was possible, or they led to other things that you hadn't even considered. Maybe there was a quality of surprise connected to them, or they were things you made happen against all odds. The broader the common thread is, the better.

What you're looking for is the consistency of how you felt in each case—who you were—not what was happening externally. For example, if you wrote down three sports examples, the commonality is not just sports or even a particular sport. Ask yourself: what exactly was the common thread of passion? Were you passionate about playing, winning, competing, or being part of a team? These are very different responses and will take you in very different directions.

The acid test is whether or not the consistent element or elements in your memories of passion were something about which you felt excited; however, don't be concerned if passion seems to elude you at first. Some people feel passion about their purpose as soon as they define it. Others might not be sure if the stated purpose is something that truly excites them. You may not experience passion until you're in action on a project; someone else might be turned on by the planning process. If you're having difficulty finding the common thread in all three accomplishments, but you were excited by two of them, you're probably on the right track.

Don't worry about trying to turn these memories into a purpose just yet. Right now, you're just looking for clues. Once I've shared all five ways you might find these clues, we'll talk about how to craft a purpose statement that captures your passion and fires up your imagination.

2. Go on a Passion Quest

A Passion Quest is a wonderful way to look in your present for your purpose. As human beings we are constantly growing and changing, and sometimes the things about which we were passionate in the past no longer turn us on in the same way. If you're having difficulty discovering your purpose through memories of past passion, try taking yourself on a Passion Quest to discover who you are *now*—including what you love, what you long for, and what no longer works for you.

A Passion Quest could take a day, a weekend, a week, or a year. You don't have to put the rest of your life on hold. The idea is simply to choose a period of time during which you will pay particular attention to what lights up your passion; then follow those threads and see where they lead you. Look for what matters to you, what moves you, even what frustrates, or angers you. And then follow it—that's why it's called a quest. Start to do the little things in life you love. If you love to cook, take a class or have a small dinner party. If you love adventure but time or money (or both) won't allow you a major vacation, consider a day hike or a weekend trip. Do the things you love, but make them part of the research phase of a project called Finding My Purpose. When I am in Passion Quest mode, I pay extra attention to how life affects me: what makes me laugh or cry, and what upsets or excites me. I notice what I am drawn to, even the movies I'm watching.

For that period of time, explore life, using passion as the barometer for deciding what you will and won't do (when choice is an option). Whether you're doing something work-related or personal, notice what excites you versus what drains you. Reignite your passion by simply doing more of what you love. Do you remember when you were a kid, playing a game in which, as you got closer to the thing you were seeking, people would say, "Warm, warmer, hot, burning hot," or as you got farther away, they would say, "Lukewarm, cool, cold, colder, freezing"? It's kind of like that on a Passion Quest. You move toward what lights you up, what gives you energy and vitality, and move away from the things that deaden you, tire you, or drain you.

It was a Passion Quest that led me to a new life and the path I am on now. Many years ago, I hit a point where I was unwilling to continue to schedule my life into thirty-minute meetings and meals. Deciding to close my marketing company I vowed to find more meaningful work and set out on a Passion Quest.

Driving home one evening, I heard a radio commercial for the Make-a-Wish Foundation, and something inside of me went "zing." Because I was on a Passion Quest, I followed that feeling—warm, warmer, hot—to a volunteer meeting. I still remember it vividly. The room was small with an exposed light bulb hanging low over a round, wooden table with paint peeling off the walls. It was non-profit land, yet the work being done in the room was priceless.

At that table, five of us brainstormed how we were going to raise money to send a young boy to Disneyland and get another child a puppy. After the meeting, I got into my car, put the key into the ignition, and began to sob. I was so inspired by who these people were and the good work they were doing that I knew at some level this was my calling. Little did I realize it, but that day was the beginning of a life dedicated to helping people achieve their dreams.

When you're on a Passion Quest, you put your antennae up and pay attention to what you need to say "yes" to and what you need to say "no" to. My Passion Quest began with saying "no" to my business that was no longer fulfilling. Remember that bringing new dreams and visions into your life often requires creating space (something we'll be talking more about in chapter ten).

Here is the essential question you are asking yourself on your Passion Quest: who am I now and what am I passionate about? The dreams you have in your fifties and sixties, for example, might be very different than those you had in your twenties, thirties, or forties. So a Passion Quest is an opportunity to meet yourself anew, to discover who you are now, rather than assuming that what you wanted before is what you still want. It's a chance to open, imagine, dream, and create how you want the next phase of your life to be.

One of the critical skills to use during a Passion Quest is what's known as "beginner's mind" or the curiosity of a child. Try to set aside all of your ideas and beliefs, and resist the temptation to jump to conclusions or dismiss anything too quickly. As soon as you say, "I know for certain . . ." it cuts off the energy of discovery. During the time you've set aside for your quest, keep exploring with an open heart and mind.

A Passion Quest is the perfect prescription for someone who is seeking to get in touch with their purpose or dreams. You can also use it to make specific life choices or decisions, like a career change or a major move. In these cases, however, you might want to set a specific timeframe around your quest.

On your Passion Quest, let life lead you to and through the unknown where amazing gifts and insights often await. Taking quality time for your heart and soul is an act of generosity. If you think it's selfish, consider this. Connected to your passion and dreams, you will have more love, joy, and energy to share with the people you love and care about most.

3. Return to Your Wound

Sometimes, as we discussed in the last chapter, the seed of your purpose can be found in your wound, or in the darkest period of your life. In fact, some of the most purpose-driven people I have met are those who have suffered the most. And they often claim that their suffering was the most important thing that ever happened to them because that's where they found out who they are and why they are here. They have, as I said, been to hell, lived to tell about it, transmuted it into love, and are here to teach about it!

You might want to return to the sacred wound exercise in the previous chapter, or you might just want to take some time to think about your greatest struggles and trials. What did you learn about yourself during those difficult times? What made them meaningful to you, even if they were painful?

Kortney Clemons found his purpose via a terrible, literal wound. As a young man, he loved sports and wanted to be part of a team. That's why he enlisted in the Army. After close to a year in Iraq, he was ready to come home to play softball. As a former U.S. Army combat medic, he was near Baghdad when he came across a soldier who'd been injured when a Humvee flipped over. While he and other medics transported the wounded man into a helicopter, a roadside bomb exploded, killing three. Kortney was lucky to live, but the explosion took his left leg from above the knee.

The twenty-six-year-old should have been discharged and back home in Mississippi five days before the attack, but the Pentagon issued a "stop-loss" order, keeping him in Iraq.

"I had to lose my leg to find the real me," he said. "I thought I had life figured out but this was really hard. I had never experienced adversity and at the end of the day it was just me and my amputation. I had to find out what kind of person I really was."

While in rehabilitation in San Antonio, Kortney met John Register, a man who would change his life. John was a lover of track and field and ran on a prosthetic leg, held the American record in the long jump, and won a silver medal in the Sydney, Australia, Paralympics, just inches shy of the gold.

"John introduced me to a new way of thinking. When you lose a limb it's easy to think you're broken or useless. If you would have told me I was going to run again, I would have thought you were crazy."

Now Kortney runs with a specially designed prosthetic "sprinting leg" that provides both balance and speed. He became the first Iraq war veteran to qualify for the U.S. Paralympic Games. He became the national champion in the "all-comers" one hundred meter sprint, with a personal record of 15.61 seconds. Kortney's dream of being an athlete is still alive, but now it's connected to a deeper purpose that he found when he lost his leg: to prove that anything is possible.

"I talk to people about being patient and in balance," he says. "Life (and my leg) doesn't work if I'm not. Everybody has a unique purpose and if you do what you're supposed to do, you will get where you are supposed to go. I'm living proof that you can accomplish anything.

"My dream? Definitely to win the gold and be an example," he says. "When I saw what was possible, I knew I could do it. That's who I want to be for others."

4. Imagine Your Tombstone

When I do this exercise with my clients, I put on my best New York accent, and pretend I'm calling them on the phone.

"Ding-a-ling-a-ling!"

When they pick up the imaginary phone, I say, "This is the New York Undertaker. It's the end of your life and we need to take care of one final detail—what's going to go on your tombstone? The good news is it's all been paid for; the bad news is that there's not a lot of space. Future generations of your family will come to see it, so it needs to serve as a reminder of who you were. And no, it can't just say, 'He was a great father' or 'She was a loving mother.' You're much more than that. It needs to speak to the Essence of who you are."

I then work with my clients to craft a simple sentence that they'd be proud to have inscribed on their tombstones. Here are some examples:

She danced through life.

He played full out.

She found humor in everything.

One of the funniest, most poignant headstones I ever saw was for a dog named Trouble. Under the name were three words: "He wasn't any."

Try this exercise for yourself. You don't have to do the accent, but think seriously about how you'd answer that call. Try to write a short phrase that sums you up. This can be a powerful clue to your purpose.

5. Direct Access

Remember, your purpose is not something outside of yourself—it already exists deep within you. It's connected to your Essence. A final technique for getting in touch with your purpose is simply to ask a trusted source within yourself. This is what Tim Kelley,

Founder/CEO of the True Purpose® Institute, calls "the direct access." Wayne Dyer, in his book *Your Sacred Self,* writes, "Inside of you there is a wise guide, a part of your true self that walks with you as you progress along the path of your sacred quest."[3] As you develop this part of yourself, you are accessing a teacher that will always be there for you. That teacher is you.

This is a more esoteric or spiritual approach, so it might not be something you feel comfortable with. But if you are someone who finds meditative or contemplative practices helpful, this might be an approach you'd like to try.

I invite you today and for the next few days to practice reconnecting with this profound part of yourself. I recommend that you slow down just a bit, take a few extra breaths, and listen for that quiet voice within yourself, your intuitive voice, that is definitely there and eager to be heard and trusted. This inner guidance and inner knowing will show you the way. It has many answers, provides wonderful insights and can add tremendous confidence and ease to your life.

One powerful technique for accessing your inner guide is to have a conversation with yourself. You might choose to relate to that inner guidance as your heart, soul, or God, if you feel comfortable with that. Whatever you choose to call it, the technique for connecting with it is known as voice dialogue work. You actually give your heart or soul a voice and sit down to have a chat, a real heart-to-heart with yourself. Ask yourself some simple, yet direct questions, and listen for and begin to write whatever answers your heart gives you. Some questions might include:

Why am I here?

What is mine to do?

How does my wound impact my destiny?

What is necessary for me to accomplish in order to die happy and fulfilled?

In your Dream Book, write down your question; then listen for the answer and write it down in the form of a dialogue. I use my initial, M for Marcia, and G for God. Here's an example:

M: Are you there, God?

G: Of course, I'm always here.

M: What is mine to do?

G: We have great plans for you.

M: Such as?

G: You've developed the capacity to believe in that which cannot be seen and is not obvious. Your tremendous faith is a gift to others.

M: What do you mean? What do I do with it?

G: Your ability to act on what is unknown will help others do the same.

M: Is that a career?

G: It speaks more to the Essence of who you are.

M: So is that a purpose, to believe?

G: Absolutely. Your purpose is to believe, which includes not only having great faith but acting on it.

M: But what do I do with it?

G: Use your life as an example to others to deepen their faith and act on what's important to them.

M: Well, I really have no idea how to do that.

G: Have faith and I will lead the way.

Sometimes you might just get one-word answers; other times a simple question will give rise to pages of insight. In this practice, your approach needs to be like that of an investigative reporter. You need to be really curious and not looking for a specific outcome. Allow the conversation to flow through you, both the questions and the answers.

Get to know your inner guide. Talk your heart out. Feel what moves you and what touches you. Let your inner wisdom help you develop a trusting relationship with yourself. Follow your intuition to your treasure and your truth.

Perhaps you will find that you connect better with that inner wisdom when you are in a beautiful place in nature. If you have a religious or spiritual path, there might be a place of worship that is meaningful to you.

The most powerful aspect of this practice comes when you actually do what that voice is saying. Take the advice it is offering. The more you hear this voice and the more you act on it, the more you will develop this part of yourself. Once you begin to follow your intuition, stop and acknowledge that's what you did. Actually say to yourself, "I listened, I acted, and it worked." Then, do it again. In developing this part of yourself, you are strengthening your "manifesting muscles" through trust.

Speaking Your Purpose

If one or more of the exercises above has resonated with you, you should be starting to get a sense of your purpose. Perhaps you've found a common thread of passion or meaning in your answers to several of the questions. The next step is to craft a statement of purpose using language that affirms your passion.

Again, don't feel you have to get it right all at once. Your purpose statement might evolve and change as you work with it. When I first started to define my own purpose, I began by simply looking at what I enjoyed doing. I decided that I liked to talk and travel, so I defined my life's purpose as "talking and traveling." But later I realized that was a dream rather than a purpose.

Over time, that description was honed and sharpened, and also broadened to make space for more possibilities. Initially, I used the first exercise above—remembering passionate moments in my life—to help me refine my purpose. One of the memories I chose was the day I won my eighth-grade speech contest. I had such fun and creatively spoke about wanting to be the first woman astronaut. The common thread I saw in this and the other memories I chose was that I was happy and freely expressing myself, so my purpose was "to joyously self-express." Later, I saw that even that was more of a dream—there was deeper for me to go. As I worked with the voice dialogue as shown above, I came upon my true purpose: *to believe.* Once you meet me (which I hope will happen soon), you see instantly that believing is who I am, and it's the purpose that informs everything I do, including how I make a living (something we'll talk more about in chapter thirteen). True purpose is usually very simple.

The more you work with your purpose, the more it will start to resonate as a unique definition of who you are and who you are passionate about being. Eventually, you will create a way to speak about your purpose that really describes it for you.

Taking a fresh page in your Dream Book, try completing the following sentence: "My life's purpose is . . ." Use your three memories of passion, or one of the other exercises, to help you. Try writing the sentence in different ways so that when you think and speak about it, you feel its underlying passion.

Now rephrase your purpose to speak it in an empowering way. Here's what I mean. If all three of your memories of passion were around making a difference, and your tombstone message was "She changed the life of everyone she met," your purpose statement might be, "to be of service." But perhaps when you read that statement, you don't feel much passion around it. Perhaps you are tired or overwhelmed, and it feels like an added burden. Adding the word "easily" to the sentence might change your experience dramatically. When you say, "To easily be of service," suddenly your passion is rekindled, and you feel that you can follow that purpose without burning yourself out.

To find your passion we looked at past memories. Now you also have the opportunity to look ahead. What qualities or adjectives might lighten up your life and infuse you with more passion? For many, adding a word like *joyously, easily,* or *effortlessly* can really make a difference.

If you're wondering how simply adding a word to your purpose statement can change your life, consider this. You are about to create dreams that are an expression of your purpose. From here you will design the plan to have what you want. The more passion you have at the beginning of the process, the easier it will be to get what you want. Create a purpose statement that will be a solid foundation upon which to build big dreams.

There are two things I recommend leaving out of a purpose statement. The first is the word "others." For example, rather than saying "to inspire others," simply say "to inspire." I believe your purpose is a quality of *being* as opposed to *doing*, which means it's something you can be anywhere, even when you're alone. As soon as you put others in your purpose, then you create a situation where any time you are alone, simply taking a walk or being with yourself, you would be off-purpose. Don't make your purpose dependent on others.

The second thing I recommend omitting is money. If it's in your purpose, then anytime you're doing volunteer work or playing with your kids you will be off-purpose. That doesn't mean you can't put money in your dreams, though. If you created a purpose statement like "to be paid well for having fun," make "having fun" your purpose and then create a dream about being paid well. The simpler and more pure your purpose is, the easier it is to live it. Your purpose is who you are, while your (many) dreams are the expression of it and the way you manifest it in your life.

It doesn't matter whether your purpose is single-focused or multi-dimensional. Imagine using the zoom lens of a camera to capture your life's purpose in the most general way. Then play with the picture until the form, sound, and feel of it is right for you.

Here are some more examples from people I've worked with. For each one, you can see the three memories, the common thread, their initial attempt at defining a purpose, and then their refined purpose statements. Notice how these final statements are more empowering and more memorable.

Name: James
Memories of passion:

1. Receiving my Certified Public Accountant's certificate
2. Being promoted to manager at work
3. Buying a dream house while selling my old home without a broker

Common Threads: Satisfaction, feeling valuable, surprising people
Initial Purpose Statement: To add value to everything I do
Revised Purpose Statement: To make a difference by being different

Name: Michelle
Memories of passion:

1. Growing my business
2. Having a special relationship with a great person
3. Raising two fabulous children

Common Threads: Creativity, connection, inspiring others
Initial Purpose Statement: To use my creativity to alter other people's lives
Revised Purpose Statement: To inspire action

Name: Jack
Memories of passion:

1. Making it to the U.S. National Racquetball Team
2. Becoming racquetball state champion
3. Striving for a professional career in racquetball

Common Threads: Winning, fun, stretching myself
Initial Purpose Statement: To go for the gold
Revised Purpose Statement: To have fun while being the best that I can be

Name: Marion
Memories of passion:

1. Having twin daughters
2. Experiences in the wilderness
3. Winning the Small Business Administration's Outstanding Businesswoman Award

Common Threads: Unexpected, Adventure, Unpredictable
Initial Purpose Statement: To experience the adventure of people and life
Revised Purpose Statement: To live life as an adventure

Once you've created a purpose statement that feels powerful, start speaking it whenever you can. Using language that incorporates your newly defined purpose into your speech will affirm your passion and move you toward having your dream. Remind yourself of your purpose at different times during your day, particularly if you're feeling stuck or frustrated. For example, maybe you have a passion for learning and your purpose statement is "To constantly be learning and growing." The next time you are stuck in rush-hour traffic and you ask yourself, "What was my purpose again? Oh, yeah, to constantly be learning," it will inspire you to listen to an audiobook or a language course and feel good that you are doing something that matters to you.

Here's one more analogy. When you know your purpose and can instantly recall it, it's like you are walking around with an electrical cord. Look for outlets to plug into so you can express your passion. Your happiness and satisfaction is back in your hands where it belongs.

How Purpose Changes Everything

Some years ago, while speaking at a Young Presidents Organization conference in Prague, I met a young man named Evan Marwell. He approached me after my speech and told me it had inspired him, so I asked him what his dream was. "To retire at forty," he declared. "And I have a plan for exactly how I'm going to do it." He struck me as an unusually driven and ambitious guy, and as founder of a successful telecommunications company he was clearly well on his way to being able to live his dream.

A few years later, Evan invited me to spend a whole day with his local YPO chapter and facilitate two retreats. As I got to know him, I sensed that despite his success (by that time he had started and sold two companies), he was still unsure about what he was really here to do. He had recently moved to California to launch a hedge fund.

On that retreat, I guided each person to discover their purpose, using the techniques I've been sharing in this chapter. Evan shared his memories of passion and it quickly became clear they had one thing in common: they all involved changing things for the better. "I'm here to be a change-maker!" he realized.

Evan left that retreat and quit the hedge fund. Now he has a new dream, born out of his purpose: to change education by bringing high-speed broadband to every single public school classroom in America. After discovering that only 30% of schools had adequate broadband, he founded a non-profit called Education Superhighway to tackle the problem. As a result of Evan's work, President Obama launched an initiative to improve broadband in schools, which he mentioned in his State of the Union Address. I received an email from Evan one day with a link to the headline announcing the president's speech. "This wouldn't have happened without you helping me to understand my purpose!" he wrote. Since then, he has successfully secured billions of dollars in federal funding to support this initiative.

Evan isn't dreaming about retirement anymore. "Once I found my purpose, I didn't really have any interest in retiring," he said. "Today, I work harder than I've ever worked in my life, I get paid nothing to do it, and I've never been happier."

Evan's story is a beautiful example of what I call "turning your life right-side up." A critical part of knowing your purpose is the passion that comes from it is the ultimate time management tool. First, when you're doing what you love, it often gets done faster. But even more importantly, you can use this process to realign your life. Rather than reacting and responding to life's demands, you can proactively create your life the way you want it to be.

When I first started doing this work some years ago, I used to say, "Every day I'm doing something that I love." Now I can say, "I'm *always* doing things that I love." My office is devoid of files, except for project files because the projects come from my dreams, which come, in turn, from my purpose. I am living a life I love, one that is filled with passion. Whenever I have extra time, which I often do, I reach for one of my project files. I love working on them because I know that doing so puts me constantly in action on the purposeful life I intentionally created for myself.

Standing in your purpose, you naturally create dreams and projects that are aligned. And someday soon, when you open your calendar or scheduling device, all you will see are the activities that are moving you forward on the dreams that are truly the expression of your heart and soul through your purpose.

CHAPTER 4
Imagine Your Possibilities

Make your dreams jealous.

—Hawaiian Airlines billboard

Now that you've discovered the passion underlying your purpose, you are ready to begin to focus on the direction in which your life will be moving. In this chapter, you get to play with your dream as if you truly believe it's possible to have what you desire, have all the goals in your life align, live a life you love, have the time to enjoy it, and start right now. Check in with yourself. Does this sound enticing or frightening?

I am talking about being open to a world of possibilities. Having possibility in your life requires that you seize every opportunity to speak the words, "It is possible," and believe them. Unfortunately, most of us have been trained to believe the things we want are not possible. To change that takes retraining. You can learn to hear yourself and educate those around you to hear the possibility in what you say, instead of asking, "Have you gone mad?" The first step is allowing yourself to explore the full spectrum of dreams you could pursue.

My techniques for this process have several advantages over other approaches. One of the benefits is that you don't have to choose having your dream in one area of your life over getting what you want in others. I often hear people lament that they could have what they want if they gave up other things, or they must work endless, tedious hours to earn the kind of money they need. I don't believe it has to be that way. However, there might be sacrifices involved. People ask me all the time, "If I use your process, will it make all of my dreams come true?" And my answer is, "Not necessarily." This process will give you clarity, but you have to decide what is important to you. You can't do everything at once. If all of your energy is dedicated to growing your professional dream, you have to be mindful about what might need to be sacrificed in your personal and family life. As you'll be learning in this book, you can design strategies and shortcuts to ensure you do the things that matter to you, but the key is being clear about what those things are and ensuring they are aligned with your purpose. But before you can do that, you need to get all possibilities out on the table.

Perhaps you're wondering about the difference between your purpose and your dreams. Your purpose is fundamental: it's who you are. Dreams are mechanisms by which to bring your purpose, deliberately, into day-to-day life. Dreams answer the question, "How do you want your life to be, in all areas?"

In a business environment, we might refer to a dream as a vision, goal, or intention. What term we use doesn't matter. What matters is that we have it. I am delighted to see many companies are using the word dream in everything from advertising to annual reports. When I hear this message, or one of these companies hires me to talk about passion and vision in the workplace, I feel this is a business that really cares about its employees and customers.

I was about to give a keynote speech to three hundred bank managers, when the meeting planner came up to me and asked, "Could you please not use the word 'dream' in your talk?" I looked at her in disbelief. "That would be impossible for me. That's what my whole talk is about!" Then I asked her what her concern was. She explained that she was worried they wouldn't get it—after all, they were bankers. I assured her I would set enough context for them to be able to relate to it.

"In business, dreaming is serious business," I told them, as I walked onto the stage. "It's a driving force for transformation. Without vision companies fail. And without our own personal goals and dreams, life becomes mundane and can stagnate. As bank managers, you are actually dream coaches (although not certified ones!) because you are in the business of helping people achieve their dreams. Whether those dreams are to start a company, buy a house, retire, go back to school, send the kids to the right college, travel the world, or a myriad of other possibilities, your job is to help them find the financial resources to succeed."

My speech was so effective that Wells Fargo bank made my book *Making Your Dreams Come True* required reading for all of their managers, truly adopting the philosophy that they should think of themselves, in one form or another, as dream coaches.

Dreams also can help eliminate those aspects of life that are inconsistent with your purpose. By measuring your dreams against your purpose, you can tell if what you've chosen will move you forward with passion to live the life you want, or whether it is more about a "should," a duty or a self-imposed responsibility. If, like me, you tend to be overly goal-oriented, this activity is not intended to turn obligations into dreams. Yes, you have to pay the rent and handle other responsibilities, but those activities get scheduled into reality anyway. Creating dreams is about getting your life where you want it to be. For instance, if you have a specific financial issue, create a dream within the economic area that expresses this. The financial dream for a person who wants to live life as an adventure might be different than the financial dream for someone who wants to be in a committed family relationship.

Developing dreams is part of the process for gaining insight into what matters or doesn't matter to you. The idea is to eliminate inconsistencies, so that these dreams will be fulfilled in support of your life's purpose. The goal is alignment.

To achieve your dream, everything from this point forward needs to be done from the perspective of your purpose. Even though you might not feel at ease yet with your stated purpose, assume that you will; the comfort from living life on purpose will follow. Just trust. Living on purpose is the most joyful and fulfilling way I know to live.

Imagination

It's time to let your desire grow and there is no better tool for doing this than your very own imagination. The eighteenth century French essayist Joseph Joubert said, "Imagination is the eye of the soul."[4] Allow your soul to express itself. Even if you think you might be a little rusty in this department, it doesn't take much to get the gears functioning again. Fine-tune your desires by being aware and creative. Get in touch with your feelings. Take some time to dream!

The secret is to have fun. If this feels serious or overly significant, it probably means you have switched gears from imagining to thinking. Avoid thinking. For many of us, this is easier said than done. But over time and with practice you will come to know there is a very different way of living that doesn't require nearly the amount of thinking and effort many of us are accustomed to.

Remember when you were a kid using your imagination, or as an adult, watching children tap into that gift? There are no limits, no rules, no right or wrong ways. Children don't have preconceived notions based on their past. Everything is new and exciting. Life is a discovery. Learn from them and give it a shot.

The two necessary ingredients for an active imagination are imaging and feeling—seeing pictures in your mind and connecting them to your feelings and emotions. The more you feel, the more real it becomes. On a certain level, your psyche doesn't distinguish between thoughts, dreams, and reality.

Here's a chance to practice. If you could be anywhere, doing anything with anyone, where would you be? If you had unlimited resources, including all the time and money you needed, what would you do? Who's living the life you dream of living? If you could order off the "a la carte" menu of life, what would you have?

Imagine the "you" you've dreamed of being. Where do you live? How do you look and feel? Who are your friends and loved ones? What do you do to fill your days, your life? What do you imagine for yourself, your community, your country, the world?

If you've never thought about these things before, now is an excellent time to start. Imagine your life, your loves, your body and soul, being nurtured beyond your wildest dreams. Imagine a world that works and one reason it works is because you had a dream, like the great dreamer, Dr. Martin Luther King, Jr., that the world would look and function a certain way.

You can play this imagination game at any level. Develop yourself as a dreamer by using your imagination to dream big dreams. Don't worry. Coming back to reality is the easy part. The English poet William Blake reminds us, "What is now proved was once only imagined."[5]

Dreamstorming

Now that you've warmed up your imagination, let's take a look at all the areas of your life in which you might have dreams. I'm sure you've heard of brainstorming—well, I call this dreamstorming. Below is a list of some areas you might want to explore initially. You don't have to limit yourself to these; select areas that are important to you. Take a fresh page in your Dream Book, write your purpose statement at the top, and then make a list of any of the areas you'd like to work on. For example, these might include:

- Community

- Education

- Family

- Finances

- Fitness

- Friendship

- Fun

- Health and well-being

- Personal

- Professional

- Philanthropic/Contribution

- Recreational

- Relationships

- Spiritual

I always like to include the category "Outrageous" for those dreams that are so big, you hardly dare to admit them to yourself.

Decide not only which areas you want to pinpoint but what there is about them that needs attention. Write this down. Perhaps your relationships are boring, and you want to establish relationships that are fun or find your dream mate. Maybe you want to become involved in your community in a more creative, innovative, or substantive way than before. Once you've created your list, review it and add anything more that comes to mind.

As you're doing this exercise, perhaps you will hear a small voice saying you can't have what you want; you don't have the time or the resources to take on anything else. Should this nagging voice of doubt begin to surface here, don't fret. We will address your doubts and concerns in Part Two of this book. Right now, you simply have to be who you say you are; you can create a whole new life from this moment forward. I want to invite you to really begin to dream, to imagine how you want your life to be, without being concerned about whether you believe you can have it or not. That's why I call it dreaming!

Ask yourself what sort of dreams a person with your life's purpose would want. Then listen for the answers. Remember that your dreams are both the way to incorporate your purpose into daily life and a tool for eliminating inconsistencies. Be sure there is no disparity between the dreams you've listed and your life's purpose. One way to do that is to role-play—to "be" your life's purpose —and ask, "If this is who I am as my life's purpose, is this an appropriate dream? Does it line up? Does it turn me on?"

Don't carry any dreams over from an "old list" or from what your parents wanted; the values you develop now are the ones by which to live your future life. You might have what I call "lingering dreams;" dreams that you think maybe, someday, you will get to. I have two potential options for you with regards to dreams like that: do it or dump it. If you've had a dream on your list for years, it's time to take a fresh look at it. Is this something that really matters to you? Is this something you still want? Or has your passion and interest in it waned? As we will discuss in more detail in chapter nine, nothing activates the voice of doubt more than something you say you want but you do nothing about. If you're not going to act on it, take it off the list. Make room for new dreams. However, if you're not ready to make that kind of clean break with your lingering dream, you could put it on a "maybe someday" list. That will prevent it from diminishing the dreams you're truly committed to.

If you develop dreams that seem contradictory, don't worry that you can't figure out right now how you're going to "have it all." Just write it all down and trust that anything is possible.

Here's a set of seemingly contradictory dreams that I often hear:

"I want a stable, well-paid job and to travel the world. And I want time to be with my partner."

Can all these things go together? Well, my brother is finding a way to prove that they can. He works for a mobile communications company that held a users' conference in Monte Carlo. He took his wife, as did the other managers. They wined and dined their customers and had a wonderful time making new friends. Monaco is filled with adventure and romance. Rekindling a little passion in his marriage certainly won't hurt his performance at work. While there, he did have to cut his playtime short one day to go back to his room for a massage and a conference call. I'm just wondering if he did them both at the same time.

Believe that it's possible to take your home life on the road, or that you can have fun at work, and you'll discover a whole new set of possibilities to enable you to have it all. Play with this idea. Keep in mind, you aren't looking for inconsistencies amongst all your dreams; you are on the look-out for dreams that are incompatible with your purpose. When you respond to the question, "Is this an appropriate dream for my purpose?" and "Are my dreams and purpose aligned?" you want to feel excited by the answer.

The Two Most Powerful Words

As a Dream Coach®, I've discovered two little words that have tremendous power: "What else?"

When you think you've listed everything that's possible, and you're sure there's nothing left, ask yourself once again, "What else is possible?" What else would bring you joy? What else would bring you fulfillment? What else would express your purpose in the world? I assure you more will come. Get in the habit of asking yourself that question, "What else?" on a daily basis, and watch as new possibilities and opportunities enter your life through opening your desires.

The American poet Audre Lorde said, "Our visions begin with our desires."[6] Your desire already exists. I hope you are feeling it as you are reading about being a dreamer, but if not, that's fine too. For now, don't think about it too much.

Never underestimate the power of your own desire. The way to ignite your passion is through your heart. Start to feel what you truly want and how you would love your life to be. Start to dream. Choose to be a dreamer and declare it. Declaration is an essential step. Clearly let yourself, others, and the universe know what it is you want. This begins your initiation to discovering and living a richer life.

The Garden of Possibility

Now that you've explored all of the areas of life in which you have dreams, I'm going to ask you to choose one category to focus on as you go through this book. When you've mastered one area by following it through to the book's conclusion, you can go back and use the same techniques to realize your dreams in the other areas of your life. This process is tried and true on all types of dreams. And if you choose to work on multiple dreams simultaneously, just be sure to follow all the steps for each one completely.

Here is a visualization exercise to help you create dreams in your chosen area of life that are consistent with your life's purpose.

Begin by closing your eyes. Take several deep breaths. Relax.

With your eyes closed, envision a beautiful garden in front of you. It's lovely and inviting, and it's filled with your favorite flowers and trees. You easily make your way in and feel so at home in this lovely place that holds your purpose.

Find a comfortable place to sit or lie, perhaps near a shady tree or next to an aromatic flowerbed. Relax; you feel completely at home, living on purpose.

It's a beautiful day; the sky is a clear blue with puffy white clouds, and the air is the perfect temperature. You're completely relaxed and at ease in your purpose, filled with passion, knowing there's unlimited possibility everywhere.

You reinforce your sense of purpose by finishing the sentence, "My life's purpose is . . ." You feel grounded in your purpose, and from that perspective, you begin to look at how you want life to be.

Keeping your eyes closed, look at the area of your life you have chosen to explore. For example, if you are focusing on the professional area, complete the sentence, "My dream in the professional area is to . . ." Perhaps you'd like to open your eyes and write it down; if you prefer to keep your eyes closed, do this when you finish.

After you've finished exploring the area you selected, relax in perfect comfort in the garden. Notice if any images or feelings come up and feel free to write them down as well. Take a last look around and experience the power that envelops you. Feel the clarity of your life's purpose, and know your dream in the area you examined is in perfect alignment with your purpose. And anything is possible.

When you're ready to leave the Garden of Possibility, breathe deeply. Relax. Open your eyes whenever you're ready. You will have a clear memory of everything that happened during the exercise.

When you've completed this exercise, you will have identified at least one dream in your chosen area. You can have more than one if you wish, but it's less important to designate many dreams than it is to be clear that the dreams express your life's purpose.

As I've said, my life's purpose is to believe. When I was in the process of redefining my career, my dream in the professional area was to have work that expresses who I am in the world. Out of this purpose, I started Dream University®, developed a Doubt Removal System, wrote fourteen books on how to make your dreams come true, and built an entire industry and brand around believing. I travel all over the world and I never feel alone. I have amazing friends. And although at the time of writing this book I'm currently not in an intimate relationship, I completely believe that I will be. As a result, I don't feel like I'm waiting or missing something. My belief makes me feel whole and complete. That's why knowing your purpose is a fundamental requirement for trusting yourself and creating dreams that are meaningful to you.

Don't be stingy when you develop dreams; put into them everything you want. When I noted that one of my dreams is to have friends worldwide, I didn't say merely that I wanted friends. I am committed to having friends everywhere on the planet, which suggests travel as another dream. If you don't develop your objectives in a way that expresses your life's purpose, your ability to make your dreams come true will be short-circuited. The power that you experience all around you comes from having passion and clarity.

CHAPTER 5
Describe Your Dream

*Why does the eye see a thing more clearly in
dreams than the imagination when awake?*

—Leonardo da Vinci

Regardless of what's going on in the world, the economy, or your own
personal checking account, there has never been a better or more important time to get clear about what you want, design it, and execute
it. And don't skip too quickly over this first element. Clarifying our
dreams is the critical component that too many of us omit, largely
because deep down we don't think our dreams are real, specific, and
attainable.

How do dreams become reality? Through projects. I'll be
teaching you how to turn your dreams into projects, with specific and
measurable results, in chapter eleven. But first, it's critical that you are
able to define and describe your dream in a way that inspires you and
gives you clues as to how to achieve it. The power to develop a viable
project depends on your ability to define your dream. Moreover, ease
will occur as new possibilities open up during this definition phase,
and you can start to launch yourself into a different dimension of
living life.

Sometimes defining a dream is as simple as choosing a date by which it will start or happen. Other times, the definition is not so simple. Having a general idea of how you want your dream to be might not be enough to know exactly how to achieve it.

Take care, however, as you move in this direction. If you jump into strategy and implementation too soon and need to have every detail spelled out, you could compromise your dream down to fit into your current reality. But if you never get specific and strategic, your dream will never materialize. Both are important, so you have to be sensitive and develop your capacity to assess what's right for you at any given moment on the journey.

Describing Your Dream to a "T"

When a dream first enters consciousness, you might not be able to see with clarity what it looks like. Often a dream starts in the subconscious and remains a nebulous idea floating around in the back of the mind. In order for your dream to come true, it is essential to get it out of your head and start fleshing out the details.

My dear friend Cara was a city girl, but as she entered the second half of life, she found herself dreaming an unexpected dream. "It started with a conversation and a horse," she told me. She and her husband Don noticed they were having similar conversations with close friends "about our shared longing to be in community together as we got older, to be vital and continue to learn, to be connected to the land, to be in beautiful, elegant homes that don't cost millions, and to be close by to each other, perhaps within walking distance." Cara and Don took note—they were hearing a common problem and a shared vision for a solution was forming, one that excited them both.

"And then along came a horse, several to be exact," she said. Cara and Don booked a summer vacation at a luxury dude ranch in Clark, Colorado. Surrounded by the breathtaking natural beauty of the Rocky Mountains, as well as elegant lodging, Cara says "I tapped into a well of happiness as I built a deep connection with the horses. It was the first time I had felt pure joy in a long time." It started the first day, she recalled, with a visit to meet a two-week-old filly.

"I crouched down several feet away from her and reached out my hand, inviting her to say hello. She approached hesitantly at first, but then put her soft nuzzle on my hand, moving to sniff the side of my face, and finally allowing a little kiss. Time stood still and my heart opened." Throughout their week at the ranch, she was in this state of joy and gratitude.

Don and Cara returned from their dude ranch experience invigorated and rejuvenated, and Cara knew she had to continue to pursue her connection to horses. On her Passion Quest, she followed the thread and it led her to discover a woman working with therapeutic horse programs, and another who had a herd of rescued horses. Visiting this woman's ranch ignited the next step in their journey. This time it was Don who formed a powerful bond with one of the rescued horses. "Don was forever changed and deeply moved by the connection they created," Cara said.

As they left that day, they learned the founder of the horse rescue was looking for a new home for her herd. "That's where it all came together," Cara explained. "What if we could create an extraordinary long-term solution for community living that integrated natural beauty, a connection with animals (and horses in particular), vital programming, and elegant housing? And what if, in the shorter term, we could create a sustainable business that integrated a first-class conference facility, with services and programming that included being with the horses and the land—a holistic planning and/or leadership development experience that enabled a new level of team creativity and interpersonal connection?" Suddenly, Cara and Don could see a pathway from the near-term vision of a business that built on their professional strengths to their longer-term vision for their dream retirement community.

Now that the vision was clear, Cara and Don realized they were almost ready to start looking for property. They sat down and took that clarity one step further, writing out a list of detailed criteria for the piece of land that would house their dream:

1. Accessibility to airport(s), hotels, restaurants and a retreat feeling

2. Views/vistas: beauty, expansiveness, and shade

3. Warm microclimate

4. Abundant water sources and utilities

5. Cellular/landline with high-speed access

6. 60 - 80 acres with pasture suitable for 30 horses

7. Zoning: commercial and agricultural

8. Homes/horse/agricultural structures on property

9. Sub-dividable to include at least 6 homes

10. Right conditions for grapes/other growing

They're now in action on their dream. After searching for the perfect place, I just heard they're about to make an offer. And it all came from following the seeds of their purpose and creating a dream that was in alignment. "The concept we have created is founded on principles that Don and I hold dearly to our hearts," Cara said. "Co-creating with our community something that has great value for all of us; listening to what is needed and owning what is ours to do; and stewarding a connection with the earth and our animal partners. We hope, too, that what we create can be a model for others and a sound reminder that abundance, sustainability, transformation, and consciousness can manifest hand-in-hand."

I love Cara's story because it models so many of the principles I teach and live myself. She found a way to have it all, to integrate multiple dreams that came from her purpose. And her willingness to get specific and describe exactly what she wants is allowing her to make her dream a reality. Cara and Don are looking ahead to their golden years with newfound excitement, as they build a place and a community that will enable them to continue to grow and learn together with the people and animals they love. I'm so personally inspired by their vision that I am considering investing and joining them.

There are many different ways to gain access to the details of your dream. Some people like to do it through writing exercises, some find it most helpful to engage in conversations with others about their dream; and others prefer talking into a recorder. One client told me she actually thinks by talking.

I hope you will use this opportunity to really dream. Take a fresh page in your Dream Book and write out all the aspects of your dream. This exercise is a powerful way to get the dream out of your head and allow it to become real. Use the exercise to get in touch with all the resources that can help to develop your dream; use it also to get a clear image of what you want and get down on paper the level of detail behind the initial statement of your dream. Notice whether you believe it's possible to have your dream, but don't let your beliefs limit you. We'll deal with your beliefs shortly.

Play with it; use your imagination; try different alternatives. Write down something that you want in your dream and, if it doesn't feel right, change it. You are the author of your own dream. Don't deprive yourself of something just because you can't have it all. Every step you take toward your dream puts you closer to your desired result. The key question answered is this: in your dream or vision, what are you creating or accomplishing?

If you aren't happy with what you write down at first, you aren't committed to leaving it there. Rewrite it, more than once if necessary. As you start to gain clarity, what gets committed to your Dream Book will begin to feel right.

The specifics of your dream might not all come in one sitting; perhaps it will take a few days, even a few weeks. You might need to seek inspiration to complete the exercise: go online and search for ideas, watch uplifting plays or movies, or even children's movies. Follow your heart on your Passion Quest to open to even bigger possibilities—dreamstorm!

10 Ways to Recognize Your Dream

How do you know whether a dream is right for you? Here are ten ways to begin to recognize your dream and some tell-tale signs to show you that you are on the right path. Use them as you explore and seek out your dream. They are designed to help you feel the important qualities that will lead you to what matters to you most.

1. **Energy and enthusiasm.** If you are excited about a potential opportunity, perhaps can't even sleep, it's worth taking a closer look. Passion is a great barometer. When you think or speak about this dream, you feel energized and alive. These feelings can be a genuine path to your desire. Take the time to investigate.

2. **Signs.** You are receiving signals, omens, or messages, whatever you call them, and it feels like someone or something is pointing you in this direction and making sure you are paying attention. Notice what's happening and don't miss the obvious ones that come while you are awake or the less obvious ones that might come while you are asleep.

3. **Consciousness.** This dream is something you find yourself thinking about a great deal. It is definitely on your mind and it is sometimes all you can think about. Even when you are engaged in other business or play, your thoughts frequently come back to this. Why do you think this is happening?

4. **Clarity and/or confusion.** You might feel completely sure or unsure that this is for you. Both are fine. Although most of us prefer clarity, the confusion could mean you're just turning it over in your mind. Confusion and fear are both often present when we are ready to make big changes in our lives. This happens when you are actively looking for, thinking about, and feeling something. Explore it further.

5. **Ease and grace.** When something just flows and seems to happen effortlessly, it often means it's the right thing for you at this time. Go with the flow. This doesn't mean you might not

hit some snags, but there's a different kind of energy around something when it's right. Learn to feel and recognize this force. Learn to move with it.

6. **Knowing and trusting.** Sometimes we know something is right "in our bones." We know because we know. Confidence is the ability to confide in yourself. Develop this place inside of you by acting on your intuition. Even if you can't explain it to others, if this feels right to you, go for it. Even in some small way, follow your intuition.

7. **Shortcuts.** When you are being fast-tracked to something or by someone and a quicker, easier way is being presented to you, pay attention. This might mean it is the right time and place for you. You might not fully understand why a particular door has opened. Peek inside and see.

8. **Connections.** When all the right people show up and synchronicity becomes evident, take a leap forward and get a closer look. Notice what relationships are presenting themselves. Everything happens for a reason and if certain people are there to play with you and it feels right, why not?

9. **Just for you.** When all of your life experiences make you the perfect person to do this project or endeavor, when it feels like this is a dream come true, take a good look and seriously consider this opportunity now. Everything you have done in your life has prepared you to be uniquely you. See how you can use all of you.

10. **Joy and abundance.** When what you are considering makes your heart sing, when the thought of this brings a smile to your face and feeds your soul, it is probably your dream.

Transform Your Environment to Reflect Your Dreams

Another way to visualize your dream is to create representations of it in your physical space. You might start with something as simple as cleaning off your desk or organizing a special room in which you can work on your dream. Another great technique is to cut out photos from a magazine that represent aspects of your dream and pin them somewhere prominent as reminders of your dream that will stimulate your imagination. I once had a cab driver who had a photo of a younger, healthier him on his visor. He said it keeps him away from late night pizza. A salesman friend of mine carries a picture of his dream yacht in his briefcase. It keeps him inspired and he often shares it with clients. It's amazing to watch him get orders because people want to support his dream. It beats "the kids need new shoes." Perhaps you want to live near the ocean or have a view of the mountains. Find a picture of what you want, put it into your reality by posting it on the bathroom mirror, and start connecting to it. If you begin to think about it as existing now, it will become real.

Some people like to create a Dream Board or collage, so they can keep visual images of what they want right in front of them. If you do this, you can also add your purpose statement, and other words that express your dreams.

Karen, a former singer whose dream was to get back to her music, committed to setting up all of her music paraphernalia and creating a space where she could write and sing. She reminded herself that she already was a singer by pulling out autographed photos of some of the people she had worked with years ago including The Platters and Jim Stafford. This process of gathering her mementos and bringing them back out into plain sight was a powerful step for Karen.

These images became a daily reminder of the memories she loved and of her current dream. When she moved her keyboard in and put up a huge music banner, it instantly transformed her office space into an environment that was an expression of her passion. It was now her music room and the place where should would initiate her dream. It was from here she made a phone call to her colleague that led to her getting booked for a recording session. And it only took her a day to create this space in her home.

Seeking Inspiration

Another great place to find out about your waking dream is from the dreams you have while sleeping. Your waking mind might be saying you don't know what you want, but your nocturnal dreams might be painting a very clear picture. No doubt you've heard this recommendation before, but it's worth repeating: place a notepad or a recording device next to your bed. Tell yourself before you fall asleep to remember your nocturnal dreams, and eventually you will. In fact, you can plant a question in your subconscious before going to sleep—"I want more information about my destiny, or this decision I have to make"—and see what comes up during the night. As soon as you wake up, write down or record everything you remember. Learn to work with the symbols. Consider painting or drawing the images. Use your curiosity to take you deeper into the mysterious, rich dream world.

You can also daydream by relaxing and letting your mind wander. Be alert to what excites you: perhaps you admire someone's beautiful office, somebody's lovely home, parts of a job someone is performing. When you are building your dream and delineating its details, feel free to include in your dream what you like about others' realities. This is one place that plagiarizing pays off.

Perhaps you're a woman who wants a beautiful new wardrobe from your favorite designers. Maybe your dream can start with something small, like an accessory or a great pair of new shoes. Make an investment in yourself and bring part of your dream into reality; you will be that much closer to having it all. If you dream of traveling around the world, but you don't have the time or money right now, start where you can. Take a day trip, go on a hike, go to a nearby lake, stream, or ocean.

Whatever you do to stimulate your mind, pay attention and notice what feels good. Relax and enjoy this process. You are creating a design for your life, letting your dream come forward and elaborating on it. Remember, this is your dream; you don't have to choose anything you don't want, or what you think you should have, or what you've always had, or what your parents wanted you to have.

Holding Your Dreams in the Palm of Your Hand

David is a television and film director who wanted to do some quick "blueprinting" of the design for his life. We were having dinner at a restaurant in Los Angeles where they used paper tablecloths and made crayons available for patrons to amuse themselves while they waited for their food. David and I got into a conversation about what made him feel passionate; then we picked up some crayons and started to design David's dream life. It was evident that David's purpose was to be creative.

He said he was excited about five areas of his professional life: producing, directing, editing, acting, and writing. We brainstormed to find a symbol that he could always keep with him to remind him of his five passionate dream areas. We decided to use the fingers on his hand. So we traced David's hand on the paper, wrote his name on the palm, and each one of the fingers became one of his five dreams. Imagine holding all of your dreams in the palm of your hand. As soon as David felt this, he had another important realization. His success in life was also in his own hands.

Coming from his purpose, David established one dream in each area he was committed to accomplishing. Then he created three or four projects in every area, each project having specific results. David was excited about the process, and the whole year was extraordinary for him; everything he did professionally fit one of those five areas. Prior to doing the exercise, David felt he wasn't moving forward on his dream. Now he had designed, organized, and described his dream in a way that made him feel powerful and get into action. Moreover, using his hand as a representation enabled David to reinforce with ease his dream and his commitment to it at any moment he needed a reminder. He now feels that his dreams are always close at hand.

I love the story of how a young Jim Carrey reminded himself of his dream of becoming a famous actor. Despite growing up poor, he'd always had big aspirations. When he made it to Los Angeles, broke and struggling to make it in the movie business, Jim recalls how every night, he would drive up into the Hollywood hills and visualize being successful. One night in 1990, he actually wrote himself a check for ten million dollars, for "acting services rendered." He dated the check Thanksgiving 1995. He put the check in his wallet and carried it with him for the next five years, and while the check deteriorated, Jim's dream only grew stronger. Just before Thanksgiving in 1995, he got a call from his agent: He'd been offered a big movie role. The paycheck? Ten million.

Is there an image, symbol, or object you could create to always remind you of your dreams? It might be a part of your own body, or something you will see every day. It might be a special piece of jewelry—a bracelet or ring with an engraving inside, a locket, or a pendant. Be creative!

Talk to Your Kids about Their Dreams

I made a new friend recently. His name is Yuval Abramovitz, and he's a big dreamer who has dedicated himself to getting other people to share their dreams. In his book, *The List*, he tells how he's encouraged hundreds of people to create and share their bucket lists and support each other in making them real. "Don't talk about your dreams; shout your dreams!" he likes to say. He told me a beautiful story about how he shared this message with his young daughter, Shira.

When Shira was about four-and-a-half years old, they were looking up at the sky one night and saw a shooting star. She closed her eyes to make a wish.

"What did you wish?" Yuval asked her.

"I can't tell you!" she replied. "If I tell, my wish won't come true."

At that moment, Yuval realized how we've all absorbed this cultural idea that if we share our wishes, we'll destroy them. We've been encouraged to keep our dreams to ourselves. He explained to Shira that this wasn't true, for shooting stars or for birthday wishes. "You need to shout your dreams!" he told her.

So Shira confided in him that she had wished for her family to be healthy. After that, she took a piece of paper and wrote a list of her dreams: to go to Disneyland, to make ice cream, to travel to Jerusalem, to be Anna from the movie *Frozen*, and to visit the sea. "We did all of those things that very summer," Yuval recalls.

Talk to your children about their dreams. And no matter what they say, be encouraging. Don't be like my friend who called me, all concerned. "My six-year-old wants to be a K-Mart checker," she shrieked into the phone. "What should I do?" I replied, "Tell her she'll make a great checker and trust me, she'll change her mind a few hundred times between now and the time she heads off to school. Call me when she wants to be a rock star and we have a real issue to address!"

When I recently spoke at a PTA meeting, a father was there with his thirteen-year-old daughter while his wife was working late at the office. After my speech, he turned to her and said, "Tell me one of your dreams." With a big smile she said, "Daddy, my dream is to be a teacher." I waited, because the logical response I typically hear to this dream is: "Teachers don't make enough money so perhaps you should consider something else."

This great dad was truly wearing his dream coach hat as he offered a heartfelt response. With an encouraging touch on her shoulder he said, "You'll make a great teacher. Anyone that has you as their teacher will be so lucky." Her face lit up. Perhaps this young girl's dream isn't about making a lot of money but rather about uplifting others and sharing the gift of knowledge. Maybe because someone believed in her and her dream, she'll grow up to write a Pulitzer Prize-winning novel. Or maybe, if she can continue to dream big enough, she'll be the one who revamps the educational system. Extraordinary things happen when we're supported in our dreams.

The point is, talk to your kids about their dreams. Encourage them, believe them, and help them explore their heart's desire. I can't tell you how many parents I've met who tell me that they regret having squelched their children's dreams. If your child wants to be a pilot, take him up to peek into the cockpit or over to a flight school. If she wants to be a filmmaker, as soon as she is old enough or it's appropriate, take her to a movie set or a filmmaking class. Say "yes" to their dreams.

What are you modeling around the dinner table when it comes to sharing your own dreams? Are you expressing what you want and showing how you are pursuing what matters to you? Or are you complaining about how much you hate your job or how bad something is and that you can't do anything about it? Kids don't miss a thing, so catch yourself in the act. You are already a hero in your children's eyes, so here's your chance to encourage them to dream and to see what's possible. And practice seeing the world through their eyes, too. Reconnect to your imagination, to your child-like curiosity, to the part of you that believes anything is possible. While you are teaching your children to dream, let them also teach you.

I was excited to speak at a company that offered a "family dream day" with me on a Saturday afternoon. Steve showed up with his daughter, Lisa. She kept her head down as he introduced her to me and then lamented, "She's sixteen and we're having our challenges. She used to be an 'A' student. Now she's running with a bad crowd, her grades are starting to slip, and she won't listen to anything we have to say.

I nodded with empathy and said, "Well, she's here. Let's see what happens."

They completed the workshop, and as they left, Steve shot me a hopeful glance. It was two years later when I received this call from him:

"Marcia, that day Lisa shared her dream with me. She wanted to be an architect. I said I would be part of her team, so together we researched architectural schools and the kind of grades she would need to get in. Needless to say, just as you teach, her dream and her reality were miles apart. But she said she really wanted this dream and would do whatever it would take. I got her a tutor, she worked hard to get her grades up, and she put her attention on her goal. It was impressive and I cheered her on. I am thrilled to report that she graduated in the top 10% of her class and got accepted into the school of her choice. More than anything, I want to thank you because we now have our daughter back and we have never been happier."

Talk to your kids about their dreams. Demonstrate that you believe in them and amazing things will occur. And while you're at it, it wouldn't hurt to let them believe in your dreams, too!

Communicating Your Dream

As you clarify and elaborate your dream, start communicating it with others. As you'll learn in chapter twelve, this is one of the most critical skills you can master, because it's how you enroll others to help you with your dream and make it come true faster. Start communicating your dream today. Don't worry if it feels awkward at first.

If you're like any one of the thousands of people that I have spoken in front of, you're probably thinking: "If I tell you my dream you might want me to do something about it. Or you might laugh at me or steal my idea. Or I might fail."

So rather than risk that happening, we keep our dreams a secret, tucked safely away under our pillow. As a matter of fact, they are often so safely hidden, that even you might forget them.

Here's a simple exercise for getting your dreams out of your head (or out from under the pillow.) In twenty-five words or less, write in your Dream Book a succinct description of your dream. This might build on the intention you set in chapter one, but now your dream has become more rich and detailed as you've written out the longer version. See how that changes the way you would write a short summary. Keep it short enough that you could say it in ten seconds or less, but try to include a couple of words that capture the vivid picture of your dream you've been painting for yourself in this chapter.

You might be surprised to discover that ten-second exercise is enough time to say as much as two or three sentences within that amount of time. For example, the words you are reading in this paragraph can be said in about ten seconds.

Write down this ten-second version of your dream, practice speaking it aloud, and then practice by speaking it to other people. If others don't understand your message immediately, revise it until they do. Here are some examples of brief, distinct descriptions:

My dream is…

- To play a significant role in the preservation of the rainforest.

- To meet my soulmate, get married on a beach in Hawaii, and have the best relationship that I can have.

- To learn a second language.

- To run a marathon.

- To retire.

- To look and feel healthier and more physically fit at 50 than I did at 40.

- To visit the Seven Wonders of the World.

- To start a non-profit that brings education to children in developing countries.

- To be on the cover of *Time* magazine.

- To homeschool my children.

- To live abroad for a year.

- To write a best-selling novel.

- To start my own business and make it the most successful company within my niche.

The expression of what you want can be simple or it can be complex. Don't spend too long perfecting it before you start getting out there and telling people about it. Their responses will be your best feedback for honing and refining your statement. Mine is *to have people speak about dreams in a new way, to believe that their dreams are something they can create.* What's yours?

Not only is it exciting to share our dreams, it's essential. In your head, your dreams don't have a chance of survival. In your head they are mixed up with all kinds of other stuff, like your "to do" list for tomorrow and all of next week, your shopping list, your agenda for the next board meeting and a slew of other things. Get it out! Write it, clarify it, speak it, refine it, and act on it.

PART TWO

BELIEVE *In Your Dream*

CHAPTER 6
Identify Where You Are

*I like the dreams of the future better
than the history of the past—so good night!*

—Thomas Jefferson, Letter to John Adams (1816)

You have begun to gain some clarity about where you want to be in life, but the road to your dreams starts with where you are right now. You can't travel that road successfully if you don't know where you are starting, or if where you're standing is made of quicksand. How can you create a strategy for where you want to go, if you don't know where you are? If you are trying to get to New York from Florida, you would obviously use a different map than if you were coming from Texas.

An honest assessment of your current situation might lead to the disappointing discovery that you're not even close to where you intend to go. Sorry, I know reality can sometimes sting, but it is an essential part of the dream formula. Your challenge is to use whatever your existing position is, no matter how far it is from the dream, as a tool to create the momentum to move forward.

I can't stress enough the importance of making an honest assessment of where you are now. Starting with inaccurate information will lead to erroneous decisions about what has to be done, and how far you have to go to reach your dream. You cannot design your new life on a strong base if you deny any part of your present existence. Get everything out on the table; list where you are with respect to each of the facets of your life. Be brutally honest, but don't become discouraged; everyone has a number of perceived impediments to having the life they want.

I typically see two types of people. The first group takes lots of action but might not even recognize the real progress they're making. The second group talks a lot, doesn't take any real action, but claims a lot of progress. Coloring your reality to be either better or worse than it is can be confusing to yourself and everyone around you, and can sabotage even the clearest strategy. Learning to accurately assess your reality is a critical step in clarifying your dream.

This is particularly important because, later in the book, I'll be teaching you a powerful shortcut skill, which has to do with people helping you. In order to do so, they must (and you must) recognize you as being trustworthy. If you're inflating or deflating the reality of your situation, this will be difficult.

No doubt you will find that you're at a different place within each aspect of your life—closer to your dream in some and farther away from it in others. That's a typical pattern. Ask yourself where you are not only with respect to your dream but with regard to your support system, your financial aspects, and your feelings. What are your concerns and beliefs? We'll look more closely at attitudes in the next chapter; right now, it's important merely to recognize that you have opinions about where you are compared with where you want to be.

If you need a clue about where to start evaluating, look back at the list you made of all the areas of your life in which you have dreams (see chapter four). These might include:

- Personal goals

- Profession

- Education

- Family

- Friends

- Heath/Well-being

- Finances

- Fun

- Recreation

- Relationships

- Fitness

- Community

- Spirituality

- Philanthropy

- Global Outreach

- And any other outrageous dream!

And any other outrageous dream! List where you are in each of the areas of your life compared to where you want to be—the dreams you identified for that area. Don't judge; just write it all down. Take each category that feels relevant to you, then make two columns: "Where I Am" and "Where I Want to Be." As you look at where you are, you are likely to hear an inner voice whispering all your limitations—all your attitudes and beliefs, concerns, fears, worries, and tales about why you can't have what you want. For example, do you worry that going for your professional dream will take more time than there is available? Are you concerned it will take you away from your family? Do you fear it would be irresponsible for you to follow your heart? Perhaps you simply don't believe it's possible to make your dream happen. For now, just notice what you are thinking and what you are feeling. We will work with all of it, one step at a time, as we progress through this together.

Write down the concerns you have in each area. Be sure to keep them to the "Where I Am Now" column. As we'll be discussing in the next chapter, people frequently sabotage themselves by putting their attitudes, beliefs, or fears into their dream. If you're putting your concerns into your dreams, your fears will become bigger and seem more real as you move closer to getting what you want. Your concerns don't belong in your dream; they're part of where you are now, not where you're going. If your dream is to be successful, and your fear is that you won't have time for friends and family, write that in the "Where I Am Now" column. Assume that, in achieving the dream, you will have all the time you desire to enjoy your success, your friends, and your family. As you will see, once the obstacles to your dream are known and recognized in the present, you can design a strategy to manage them. Just knowing this can provide some relief and peace of mind.

Documenting of where you are as compared to where you want to be is an effective exercise. Reread the exercise or make a recording of it that you can play back whenever you want to ensure that where you want to be is clearly defined and devoid of your fears about getting there.

Tension Can Be Useful

The difference between where you are and where you want to be can create a dynamic tension. As you look at your two columns, can you feel it? The challenge is learning to use this tension as a creative force. Can you be more committed to where you want to be than to where you are? Picture the tension in a rubber band as you pull on it and the release of tension as you relax the pull. Tension will resolve itself naturally in whichever direction there is more focus. Therefore, all things being equal, something will move in whichever direction it is pulled harder.

Thus, if you put "where you want to be" (your dream) at the top of the rubber band, and place "where you are" (your reality) at the bottom of the rubber band, the difference between where you are and where you want to be will create tension. The direction in which you pull harder is the way the rubber band is going to snap. If you tug it intensely toward where you want to be, it will snap in that direction; if you pull it toward where you already are, it will snap back.

Once again, the bottom line is this: on a day-to-day basis, are you more committed to your dream or to your reality? The evidence will be clear to you in the action you are taking or not taking, in what you are doing or not doing.

If you know with clarity where you want to go, you can focus your attention on your dream and use the information about where you are to propel you forward. If you find that you're far removed from your goal, don't despair; the tension in the distance from where you are to where you want to be might launch you even faster in the direction you choose.

You can't be thrust forward, however, unless you stay clear and honest about your current position. When you start to negotiate with yourself—"Oh, it's not so bad; I've been here for a couple of years, a little while longer won't hurt"—you dilute or eliminate the dynamic. It's the tension that moves you forward.

Problem Solving

There's one kind of energy involved when you are moving toward what you want and another when you are moving away from what you don't want. For instance, you might have a problem with debt. If you just take action to eradicate the debt, you're likely to stop taking action as the problem starts to go away. Your inaction can then lead right back to the problem. Manipulating the problem always leads back to the problem. However, if you are moving *toward* a dream of financial abundance and a sustainable lifestyle, you'll naturally take care of your debt in the process and keep moving forward.

To avoid simply manipulating the problem, set up your life so that you're always moving toward what you want. For example, someone might be twenty pounds overweight. If she simply tells herself she has to lose that extra weight, she might make good progress for awhile, but studies show that in most cases, as soon as the weight begins to drop, the food intake tends to increase and the exercise tends to stop. If, on the other hand, her dream is to be healthy and vibrant, to feel and look good, a different kind of energy will be applied to the drudgery of getting rid of the weight by diet and exercise. I've seen the power of this shift myself. There was a time when, if my scale showed I had dropped a few pounds, I would go looking for brownies, until I realized this was a vicious and energy-draining cycle. If your dream is to be physically fit and your reality is you are overweight, you can tell which one you are more committed to by what you are putting in your mouth or doing in your exercise regime.

George had been severely overweight, but through great effort and perseverance he had trimmed down and he was feeling great about being healthy. When he came to me, his dream was to stay physically fit, but he was having trouble getting himself motivated to go to the gym three times a week.

In exploring George's life we discovered that his passion was to live life as an adventure. To George, that meant trying new things, seeking new challenges—in short, he hated feeling bored. Out of his enthusiasm for testing himself in new situations, he designed a project that would allow him to fulfill his dream adventurously. The project he took on was to train for a triathlon. The venture had him feeling turned on, lit up, passionate, and he had no difficulty getting to the gym with regularity. He even hired a coach to help him break through any limitations. The more George pushed himself beyond where he was, the more passionate he became. This is inherent in his purpose, to live life as an adventure. He's not focused on the problem of extra weight—he's focused on the dream of being a triathlete.

Here's just a quick note for you: if your dream is to be in great shape without having to go to the gym, this need not be considered a fantasy. My strategy for exercising without daily visits to the gym included taking up skiing and roller blading (with lots of appropriate padding) at the age of forty.

As these examples show, the critical question becomes whether you're more committed to remaining where you are or to getting where you want to be. The difference between the two is what will propel you forward.

CHAPTER 7
Deal With Your Doubter

I merely took the energy it takes to pout and wrote some blues.

— Duke Ellington

Do you ever feel like there are multiple people living inside your head, each with a different voice and opinion? Are parts of you saying "yes," while other parts are holding you back? Hearing voices doesn't make you crazy—it just makes you human. There is a cast of characters that live inside of us all and at different times we might be run by one voice over another. Most people experience themselves as having many different parts, and those parts don't usually agree with each other.

When it comes to making your dreams come true, there are four particular aspects of the self that you need to become familiar with. I have respectfully dubbed these the Dreamer, the Doubter, the Realist, and the Visionary.

The Doubter voice is often heard saying such things as, "I don't think that's a good idea." If you were to really crank the volume up on this voice it might say, "Are you out of your mind?"

The Realist says, "Be realistic." If we turn the voice of the Doubter down a bit, it becomes the voice of the Realist. Realists aren't bad; as a matter of fact, they are important, as I'll be explaining in this chapter. However, if you are overly realistic you might kill the passion around your dream.

The Dreamer says, "What if…?" The Dreamer imagines what might be possible, believes in the dream, and finds creative outlets. The Dreamer is an opportunist, always open for new potentials.

The Visionary is the voice that says, "Anything is possible; let's dream big!" If you turn up the voice of the Dreamer, it becomes the Visionary. We'll be returning to this voice in the final chapter of the book, when I invite you to dream your biggest dream. For now, however, let's focus on the voice that can most easily sabotage your dreams: the Doubter.

When you decide to pursue your dreams, the Dreamer is often gung-ho while the Doubter can provide a laundry list of concerns and issues. If you've gotten this far in the book, I'm sure you've encountered each of them at different moments as you completed the exercises in these pages. In fact, you've probably encountered both at once, and I wouldn't be surprised if they're having a heated debate.

One such moment for me occurred after I'd given a speech in Rome. A woman with a beautiful accent asked me to tell her one of my personal dreams. Assuming I'd never see her again, I decided to share a dream I had never spoken out loud, one I had done so well at keeping secret that even I had almost forgotten it.

"My dream is to spend the summer writing in the Greek Islands," I said all in one breath.

She handed me her card and replied, "I have a villa in Greece. Why don't you come as my guest?"

I was reminded that amazing things happen when we share our dreams. I was elated—or more accurately, part of me was. Here's a peek inside my head at that moment:

Dreamer: I am so excited!

Doubter: But what if she turns out to be crazy or the place is dreadful? I don't like this at all. It's far away and could be dangerous.

Dreamer: Nonsense. This is my dream handed to me on a silver platter.

Doubter/Realist (they're close cousins): Who is going to run your business while you're away?

Dreamer: My fabulous team whom I completely trust.

Doubter: Well, how's it going to look to your clients that you are out of the country for three months?

Dreamer: I think as a Dream Coach®, it's going to look pretty good.

Does that sound familiar? The Doubter's favorite phrase is "But, what if?" Here are a few more examples you might hear inside your own head:

But, what if I . . .

> . . . don't really know what I'm doing?

> . . . go for my dream and fail?

> . . . run out of money?

> . . . disappoint others?

> . . . embarrass myself?

I'm sure you can add to the list from your own particular repertoire of doubts and worries. Often as we open up to our dreams, the Doubter and its close cousin, the Realist, are waiting in the wings, wanting to know what the plan is. If you're not careful, your Doubter will sabotage your dreams with its ever-so-reasonable objections. It's essential that you learn to deal with your Doubter. If you never deal with your doubt and you meet another Doubter on the road, their doubt will magnify yours. However, if you have worked with your own doubt, next time a Doubter challenges you, by contrast it will be the opportunity to deepen your commitment and conviction to your dream.

So how do you deal with your Doubter? Many people would say, "I just try to ignore it, or turn down the volume." Here's the problem with that approach. If you turn down the voice of the Doubter, it just becomes the Realist, the part that wants to know where the time and money will come from for your venture. Eventually, if you turn it down enough, it becomes unconscious, and that's when it's actually the most dangerous, because it will sabotage your dream without you even knowing it.

I've spent thirty years developing my Doubt Removal System and it works! Here's the secret: the Doubter is not your enemy. In fact, it has valuable information that can help you achieve your dream. It will help you identify the obstacles to your dream, so that you can design strategies to overcome them. So before you turn the volume down on that voice inside your head, how about learning from it?

Let's get to know your Doubter by interviewing it and being curious. Capture its needs, insights, and wisdom by completing these sentences as your Doubter. You can either write them down or speak them out loud. Rather than just taking the first answer that arises, allow more to come by going through the questions several times:

"The way I sabotage (your name)'s dream is _____."

Example: "The way I sabotage Jenny's dream is by having her doubt herself and quit."

"When I am running (your name)'s life, I _____."

Example: "When I am running Jenny's life, I keep her too busy to focus on what's important."

"What I need from (your name) is _____."

Example: "What I need from Jenny is for her to have faith, to get help, to breathe."

The Doubter is not something to fear. It's the voice of prudence and it has insight and wisdom. Yes, it can derail you if you allow it to take over, but if you can put it in its appropriate place, it can actually become a valuable member of your team.

So let's hear some more from the Doubter. Take a clean page in your Dream Book and write down your dream in as much detail as you can. Then draw a line beneath it, and write "Current Reality." Now, write down a list of all of your doubts, fears, and hesitations. Get every obstacle you can think of out of your head and onto the page.

What you'll notice is this: every obstacle falls into one of two categories. It is either an internal limiting belief or it is something external that requires a strategy or a plan. For each item on your list, ask yourself: is it a *belief* or something that *requires a strategy*? The good news is that you can deal with both of these categories. We'll be talking about how to deal with limiting beliefs in chapter eight, and in chapter eleven, I'll be teaching you how to devise strategies to deal with even the most seemingly impassable obstacles.

Here's a sample list:

- I don't know how. (Belief and strategy)

- I'm afraid I will fail. (Belief)

- I don't have the money. (Strategy)

- I'm too tired. (Belief and strategy)

Freedom comes as you appreciate the wisdom and insight of the Doubter, rather than judging it as the enemy. As long as you don't fall into the Doubter's traps, you can utilize its realism to help make your dreams more real. And to help you keep the Doubter in its appropriate place, I'm going to share what I discovered about how we fall prey to the Doubter and sabotage our dreams.

The #1 Way We Sabotage Our Dreams

The number one way we sabotage our dreams is by projecting fear and doubt into them. What's the alternative? Keep the fear and doubt in your present reality, acknowledge and listen to it, but don't let it into your dreams. Otherwise, when you move toward your dreams you'll be moving toward your doubts. If you project your worst nightmares into your dreams, then you'll unconsciously keep them at arm's length. That's why, in the exercise above, I told you to draw a line under your dream, and place all of your doubts, fears, and worries under the heading "Current Reality."

Now ask yourself, are you more committed to your Dreamer or your Doubter? Are you more committed to your current reality or the future of your dreams? If your worst fears are included with your dream, you'll most likely be more committed to your current reality because it feels safer. It's good to listen to your Doubter, but always be sure to keep its list of obstacles within your current reality. Don't let fear and doubt inside your dream, or they'll shrink it down to accommodate them.

One Exit Too Soon

If you recognize a pattern of self-sabotage in one area of life, chances are you might be doing it in other areas as well. Paula told me that one day she noticed how when she was driving on a highway, she would frequently panic, feeling like she passed by her exit. The voice of her Doubter would tell her, "You've gone too far! You must have been distracted and missed the sign. If you don't turn back now, you'll be late!" When this happened, she would get off, turn around and go miles back, only to find she had not yet reached her exit.

She was getting off the highway one exit too soon. Knowing that she had this tendency, she learned to continue one more exit beyond where she thought she should get off. She learned to adjust her internal clock and have more patience and self-trust.

Then she asked herself, "Where else am I getting off one exit too soon or rushing through life?" Her answer was a resounding, "Everywhere."

When you catch yourself in the act of doing something that doesn't serve you, you can choose to change it. I'll be teaching you more about how to create personal practices to shift your most stubborn behavior patterns in chapter nine. When you can see a pattern and recognize the particular strategy your Doubter uses to derail you, you can shift how you live your life.

Don't Let Fear Stop You

When someone shares a dream with me, my three favorite Dream Coach® questions are:

1. What are you doing to move that dream forward?

2. What's stopping you or where are you stuck?

3. How I can help you?

Goldie told me, "My dream is to be the Mrs. Fields of Biscotti."

"Great dream," I replied. "What are you doing to move that dream forward?

"Nothing," she responded.

"Why? What's stopping you?" I asked with genuine interest.

"I'm afraid."

"Of what?"

She turned her gaze to the ground and admitted, "That no one will buy them."

I had tasted her delicious cookies and knew the perfect strategy to get her unstuck. I just wasn't sure she'd like it, and more importantly, that she'd go for it.

"Goldie," I smiled. "How many cafes would you be willing to take your cookies to next week to try to get orders?"

She looked at me with dismay. "I can't believe you're doing this to me," she said with a huff, folding her arms tightly across her chest.

"I'm supporting you." Staying firm, I repeated, "How many?"

"Okay," she snapped. "I'll take them to three cafes, but that's it and don't push me."

One year later, Goldie's Biscotti was being sold in more than fifty cafes in California and she had met with a national distributor. Her hobby-turned-business is already generating enough income to start a scholarship fund to send her daughter to college. With that first essential step beyond her fear and doubt, her business was launched.

An Unexpected Gift

Imagine there's a gift in your life, one that's so obvious that every time it shows up, it's a direct sign you're on the right path to getting what you want. Fear can be this gift, and this is how it works.

Everyone's life is about change. Sometimes *you* change, and sometimes something can change your life. Often when you think you have everything figured out, something unexpected happens, and the course you were on is somehow forever altered. As a sign on a tip jar in my local coffee shop said, "If you fear change, leave it here." Don't we wish it could be that easy?

The truth seems to be that some people fear change, some people resist change, and some rare people claim to thrive on it. Most human beings seem devoted to consistency as a way of life. Yet the only constant in life is change. What you fear might not revolve around what is being changed; what you call fear and associate with a negative belief might be your body's resistance to the act of changing.

You can learn whether you're on the right path to where you want to be by facing fear and acknowledging it as a landmark for change. That's the gift. If you were not moving away from your current identity, if you were not seeking to change your life, you would not be experiencing fear.

Because we think of change as filled with murky unknowns, the ultimate fear might feel like death. However, the experience is only the old you dying away and allowing you to be transformed. This is good news. By trusting what you want, often you will be able to release the part of you that is afraid of making your dream come true. By shedding the pieces that no longer fit, you can create a new dream to move toward. Fear is actually a measurement tool; it means you're leaving the old and out-of-date behind you; it's a gift that indicates you are closer to your dream. In this way, fear can be seen as a healthy and natural mechanism, a sign of vitality and evidence that you are in process. Sadly, unless you learn to use fear as empowerment, it can also stop your progress dead in its tracks.

First you need to be able to distinguish fear that protects from fear that restricts. When fear keeps you out of dark alleys at two o'clock in the morning, you would do well to listen to that inner voice. On the other hand, fear of change, fear of moving closer to a dream, or fear of something you've always wanted is negative and limiting.

Suppose you always wanted a little country home. You've dreamed about the rooms, the yard, the picket fence. One day you find your dream home and you think, "Oh Lord, now what?" The thoughts that fly through your mind create fear and you invent stories to justify why you're afraid.

"I just can't give up my friends and move away."

"I'll never sell my house."

"It's too small (or too large) for me."

"The commute will be too far."

"No one will visit me out there."

"It was only a dream anyway."

Take a fresh look at the dream. Start by closing your eyes and reconnecting with the dream house. Assume there are no limiting circumstances like the ones listed above, and ask, "Is this the house of my dreams?" If the answer is "no," you can let it go. If the answer is "yes," then you can go for it. Feel what's true in your heart.

Does facing your fear automatically ensure it won't happen? Of course not. However the situation turns out, what matters is the meaning you give to the outcome. Will a negative result mean that you're a failure and that you shouldn't go for your dream? Will you be able to accept the outcome, whatever it is? I hope you won't be someone who uses the demise of a dream to stop dreaming altogether.

When it comes to dreams, I don't know any better way to build self-confidence than to articulate a dream that is important to you, put it out to the world, and give it all you've got. Do we ever fail, fall short, or have disappointments? Of course we do. It's called life and learning. The true test of character is what you do in the face of a setback. Will you take stock, check in, and try something new? Or will you give up or even worse, stop dreaming?

It's Never Too Late

Bessie had been an amateur photographer for twenty-five years. Now at seventy, she had a very clear dream.

"I want to be a world famous, professional photographer," she said and then emphasized, "The difference between an amateur and a professional is a professional gets paid."

"Fabulous," I exclaimed. "Is anything stopping you?"

She paused for a long time. "I'm sure I need credentials but don't want to go back to school at my age."

I listened between the words and felt what she wasn't saying. "Bessie, what's really in your way?" I gently asked.

"Everyone is telling me I am too old," she slumped. "They're telling me to be realistic."

Outrageous, I thought. "Nonsense," I said. "What's a step you can take to show that you are more committed to your dream than to their doubt?"

She reflected for a moment and then suddenly her eyes lit up. "I know what I can do. I have an application sitting on my desk for a photo contest sponsored by Kodak. Just entering would have me prove to myself that I am serious about this."

She took a stunning photograph of a man playing a sousaphone with golden tones of his instrument reflecting his bright red band uniform. She proudly sent it off to the Kodak competition, along with five hundred thousand other entrants.

Bessie won first prize, which included a check for ten thousand dollars. "I ran out to get business cards printed," she bragged. "After all, now I really am a professional."

Her photograph toured around the world with the *Journey into Imagination* exhibit. She got the whole dream.

"Bessie, what did you learn from this? What wisdom would you share?" I asked.

She looked me square in the eyes and said, "It's never too late to make a dream come true."

Until you get to the end of your life and look back on what you did or didn't accomplish, how do you know if something is realistic? Most people compromise their dreams down to what they realistically believe they can accomplish before they explore the possibilities of where their dreams might take them. Not Bessie—and not you!

CHAPTER 8
Transform Your Beliefs

We don't see things as they are; we see them as we are.

—Anaïs Nin

One day, while working out at my health club, I saw a handsome man in his late thirties just sitting on a Nautilus machine, staring into space.

Jokingly, I said, "C'mon, aren't you here to work out? Get going!"

He looked up at me, his face serious, and said he was thinking about the year ahead and about some goals he had set.

"Like what?" I asked. I'm always ready to hear people's goals and dreams, and in my thirty years as a Dream Coach® I've heard some pretty far-fetched ones. It's hard to surprise me, but Greg's answer took me aback.

"I plan to be walking by the end of this year," he replied, as he crawled off the machine and reached for the wheelchair I hadn't noticed.

Greg explained that he had been in the wrong place at the wrong time, got caught in crossfire and was shot in the leg. His doctors thought it was a miracle that he lived through the night, and they told him and his family that he would never walk again. Greg believed them.

However, one day, while Greg lay in a hospital bed feeling the futility of his situation, his toe moved. "It just moved," he told me. The doctors assured him it was nothing, just nerves; but, for Greg, it was the beginning of a new belief. The expectation that he would walk again became the driving force of his life, and he became passionately committed to turning his dream into reality.

I saw Greg recently. Not only was he walking but he was eager to share his new dream.

"My next step is to find myself a girlfriend and take her dancing. But my five-year goal is to run a marathon. Pretty unbelievable," he chuckled, "for a guy who was told he would never walk again."

Whose beliefs are you buying? What's stopping you from going for your dreams? Anything and everything you want is no more than a belief away.

Choose Your Beliefs

I'm sure I'm not the first person to tell you that your beliefs either hold you back or move you forward. Since your attitudes and beliefs determine the choices and decisions you make, your beliefs will either empower or impede you. But what you might be forgetting, as many people do, is that you can choose what you believe. Greg chose to believe in his own dream, not what his doctors told him.

Our beliefs are our own opinions and judgments, or the opinions and judgments we've inherited from others, but for some strange reason, we seem to forget we can choose them. In any given moment and in any given circumstance, we choose what we believe. Just keep in mind, if you choose a positive belief, you will move forward on your dreams. If you choose a limiting belief, you won't. You'll probably get stuck or sabotage your goals.

When you are not consciously choosing to believe an empowering belief, what you get by default is your old limiting beliefs. We are deeply programmed. If you are not thinking "yes," some part of you is already acting on "no." Learn to manage your mind by noticing the choices you are and are not making. Ask yourself, "Why am I doing this? What am I believing?" The answers might astound you. Are your beliefs serving you? Become suspicious of your default settings.

Sometimes beliefs are formed by personal experience; other times they come from the culture around you. During my recent visit to Israel, I noticed a lot of the people I was coaching would start describing their visions with phrases like, "It's complicated..." or "You don't understand because in Israel..." I'd only been there a few days and heard this often. They must have been hearing it their whole lives—and they clearly believed it. Finally, I asked, "Aren't you tired of that story? Isn't it time for a new story that's about creating what you want as opposed to dwelling on what's not working and being stuck in the past?" I know this is a bigger conversation and unraveling collective beliefs sometimes takes time, but I got a standing ovation so it seems that many people are ready for a real change.

What does it take to change a limiting belief to a positive one? You can't just say, "I believe!" and wave a magic wand. To move from an old limiting belief that will hold you back to a new empowering one that will be the foundation for the life of your dreams takes some work. But it's a critical skill and worthy of your time and energy. Here are the three keys to transforming your beliefs: willingness, courage, and practice. It takes willingness to choose a new empowering belief, courage to act on it, and practice to do it again and again until your reality shifts and your trust in yourself deepens. And it will.

Grasp this concept and you'll have access to one of the most powerful tools for impacting your reality.

Everyone has attitudes and beliefs about the various aspects of their lives. Your opinions are long-term parts of who you are and they've been developing for as many years as you've been alive. Human beings are meaning-making machines, constantly interpreting our experiences and the world around us, and assigning meaning to things and experiences. This is how we make sense of our world, but it becomes a problem when we give too much meaning to the wrong things, or interpret events in ways that form limiting beliefs. Many of us seek meaning in the wrong places; we allocate it to external things, such as fame, accomplishment, or material objects. We habitually think in ways that limit us, restrict us, and hold us back, while we miss the beauty and wonder of life.

We see this often when people have made mistakes, suffered loss, or been betrayed. They interpret these events as meaning something about them, and they form a belief that they can expect more of the same. If you did the sacred wound exercise in chapter two, you will have seen a powerful example of this, and looked at how your belief can shift from victimization to empowerment. What other experiences in your life have you interpreted in such a way as to form a belief about yourself? Are those beliefs working for or against your dreams? Are they encouraging or inspiring you to take greater risks, or are they causing you to play it safe and seek certainty? The meaning we assign to a single event can be liberating or devastating. Take a moment and check in with the pivotal moments in your life. What meaning did you consciously or unconsciously assign to them, and what's another perspective you could adopt right now?

Attitudes and beliefs can be negative or positive, but need not be barriers to achieving what you want. Either way, it's possible to use them to your advantage, but first, identifying them is critical.

The decisions and choices you make ultimately result from the attitudes and beliefs you hold about everything in your life. The process looks like this:

Your Attitudes & Beliefs

create

Your Thoughts & Feelings

which determine

Your Choices & Decisions

If you want to become aware of your attitudes and beliefs, one clue is to pay attention to what you're thinking and feeling. For example, if your dream is to establish a new career, but every time you think about it, you feel futility and hopelessness, those feelings are clues to your deeper belief, which might be that it's not possible, or that you don't deserve it.

Once you unearth the belief, you can replace it with a new one. Your thought process can become, "I think I can make this happen," and "I think I know who can help me," or "I do deserve a new career and I'm going to prove it by working hard to make it happen."

Simply changing your belief has shifted your internal conversation from thinking of your dream as impossible to seeing its possibilities.

Attitudes and beliefs are at the core of how you react in the world. No matter how or why you developed them, it's crucial you take responsibility for them, and you evaluate them honestly. The naked truth about your attitudes and beliefs in this chapter is as important as your honest assessment in chapter six of where you are versus where you want to be.

For example, you might believe you can't have what you want, or you can only get a portion of it, or that getting what you want will create more problems so it's better not to try. You might believe you're facing barriers you can't move beyond: your gender, genes, education, or work experience. Look back at the list of obstacles you made when you were listening to your Doubter. How many of them fall into the category of "attitudes and beliefs"?

Attitudes and beliefs are never neutral. They either move you forward or hold you back. Beliefs that are positive are your allies; they're on your side as you design the life you want. Those that are negative can sabotage you, especially if they're perceived as the biggest part of where you are now, or if they get inserted into your dream (remember, that's the number one way we sabotage our dreams). Unexamined negative attitudes can become bigger than your dream and turn into insurmountable obstacles after you're already on the road to what you want. If you dream of a life of ease but you don't believe it's possible, watch how quickly you'll prove yourself right. But if you take the same dream—to have a life of ease—and act as though you believe in it, you will take different actions. If we don't believe in our dreams we either abandon or sabotage them. If we do believe, we'll at least begin the process of seeing where the dream will take us. Many people live in an evidence-based reality. "I'll believe it when I see it," is a comment I often hear. But what if the opposite is true? What if you won't see it until you believe it?

Often we kill off our dreams before we ever explore their possibilities. Perhaps our past defeats or disappointments rear their ugly heads. We might think, "I failed at this before. Why should I try it now?" Do you use your past failures to deny your dreams? Or worse, do you use past memories as the justification for not dreaming at all? If we are not aware of our limiting beliefs, they can be deadly. They kill our dreams.

Here's a roster of the limiting beliefs I hear most frequently:

- I don't have the time, money, resources, skills, or knowledge.

- I'm not successful enough; I'm not good enough.

- I'm too successful, too young, too old, or too resistant to change.

- I'm in the wrong geographical location.

- I don't have any knowledge in that area.

- I missed my opportunity years ago and it's too late.

- My energy is too low.

- It's too hard, too technical for me.

- I don't think I can learn what I need to know.

- I don't trust myself or anyone else.

- I worry about what others will think.

- I don't believe it's possible, so why bother?

Do any of these sound familiar? If you look closely at your own beliefs, you might notice they tend to fall into one of three basic categories that are common to most human beings. I call these Inadequacy, Scarcity, and Mistrust.

Inadequacy means "I'm not _____ enough." You can fill in the blank. I'm not good enough, smart enough, fast enough, rich enough, thin enough, young enough, old enough, etc. At a workshop I gave in Baltimore, one young woman had written more than three pages of limiting beliefs that she recognized herself as having. After a discussion, she saw that the majority of them fit into one category: inadequacy. By noticing this theme, she was able to make a huge attitude shift with a little bit of work.

Scarcity means "there's not enough _____ to go around." This could be time, resources, love, energy, support, or you. The most common expression of the scarcity belief is "there's not enough money," which I'll return to in a moment.

Mistrust means "I don't trust _____." It could be yourself, someone else, the weather, the timing, the process, or the unknown. Maybe you just don't trust anything or, for that matter, anyone. Can you see how challenging it is to have dreams, much less to act on them, if you don't trust? We'll be returning to the topic in chapter fourteen, but for now, notice whether any of your beliefs fall into this category.

As you begin to unearth your limiting beliefs, you have the opportunity to choose new ones. Remember, it takes willingness, courage, and practice. Here are some alternative beliefs to correspond with those listed above:

- I *do* have the time, money, resources, skills, or knowledge.

- I'm successful enough and good enough.

- I'm old enough, young enough, and flexible enough.

- I'm in a good geographical location.

- I can accomplish this anywhere.

- I have the knowledge in this new area.

- I have a good opportunity before me now.

- My energy is high.

- I believe in me.

- I can learn what I need to know.

- I have no worries about what others will think.

- It's the perfect time.

- I believe it's possible.

The Big Book of Your Beliefs

Here's a visualization exercise for changing your beliefs. Find your-self a quiet spot and relax. Take several deep breaths and prepare yourself for a journey into your mind. Imagine that you're in the attic of your mind. It's filled with lots of dusty memories: your bicycle from when you were three, your mother's wedding dress, old photo albums.

As you walk through the attic, you come to a corner. In the corner there's a beautiful pedestal on top of which is a big book. On the cover of the book it says *My Beliefs*. Blow a little dust off of the book, open it, and turn to a page where you have a belief you want to change.

See your belief on that page. You can write it in your Dream Book if you like or just picture it in your mind. For example, "It's not possible to achieve my dream," or "I am inadequate." Whatever that old belief is, read it and prepare to change it.

Read that belief from the page in the book, and then in your mind's eye, take a big, black marker and draw a huge "X" through it. You can even do this in your notebook if you like. Then visualize yourself tearing the page out of the book and burning it. Get rid of that belief. Feel the emotion of finally letting this old belief go.

Now you're left with a clean page in the book because there was nothing behind the page you tore out. Pick up a new magic marker in your favorite color and write your new belief. Your new belief will correspond to the one you destroyed, and it will be stated positively and in the first person: "It is possible for me to achieve my dream," or "I am more than enough." You might even consider adding the word "easily."

Write your new belief expressively and with flair so that you feel it and can internalize it. After you've written it, read your new belief out loud to yourself. Then close the book, leave the attic, and know that your new, positive attitude now lives in The Big Book of Your Beliefs.

Do you believe you changed your belief? Do you at least believe that it's possible you changed it? Or do you believe it can't be that easy? What if it is that easy? It's all up to you. You decide whether to believe or not. That's how beliefs work. What makes it real is what you do with it. Acting upon a new belief shows that you really do believe it.

Four Common Beliefs that can Sabotage Your Dreams

Sometimes your limiting beliefs can disguise themselves as truths. Here are four tricky ones that could sabotage your dreams if you're not careful, and suggestions for how you could reframe them.

Belief #1: "I'm confused."

Many people allow themselves to be derailed by the belief that they are confused or don't know how to proceed.

Suggestion: "As I get clear about my dream, I will know what to do." Ask yourself, "What can I clarify about my dream?" Being vague about your dream will keep you confused. If you do not have clarity about your dream, it's difficult to know what to do about it or ask anyone for help. Don't let the belief "I'm confused" throw you off-course. Go back and clarify your dream, practice writing it down and speaking it out loud.

Another suggestion for replacing that belief would be: "I'm in a creative process." Perhaps you have a belief that confusion is always bad, when, in fact, it might just mean that you're in the middle of a transition, opening yourself up to the unknown. Hold steady and allow yourself to trust what is unfolding, and don't let your limiting belief close up the doors of opportunity and new potential.

Belief #2: "I don't need to do anything, all I have to do is trust and wait."

This is a common belief that is even perpetuated by many teachers who claim to help people manifest their dreams. But it's a belief that will set you up for inevitable disappointment, and disappointment can cause you to give up or not be able to see new opportunities or other solutions.

Suggestion: "I have the power to make my dreams come true through action." This is a much more empowering and inspiring belief than the one above. Make a plan. Be realistic on strategy. Turn your dream into a project or projects, and take it one step at a time. Look at what else is happening in your life and learn to schedule creatively and efficiently. Use your time wisely. Set up a simple system so you can see that you are making progress. If you keep doing the things necessary to get the project done, it will happen.

Belief #3: "It's so much easier to do it myself."

Too many of us hold on to the mistaken belief we can do it alone. As busy as you are, if there's an easier way to make your dream happen, don't you want to know it? Are you sabotaging your dream by declaring you are the only one who can do all the things it will take to get the job done, while complaining you just don't have the time to do them, so therefore nothing is happening?

Suggestion: "Other people can help me to manifest my dream faster." Get help. Enroll other people in your dream and get them excited about helping. I'll be teaching you more about how to do this in chapter twelve. At the very least, identify one person who will support you in making this dream happen. It could be a great buddy or spouse who will support you by holding you accountable for doing the things you said you would do. The single most powerful thing you can do to make your dream come true is share your dream with someone who is on your side.

Belief #4: "I have to pursue my dream at any cost."

This can seem like a noble belief, but it's actually destructive. After all, if you kill yourself in the process, you won't get to enjoy the dream. The worst thing that could possibly happen on the road to your dreams is you forget about taking care of yourself. If you sell out on your own well-being in order to make the dream happen, you will suffer and so will the dream.

Suggestion: "My well-being is critical to the pursuit of my dream." Your body, mind, heart, and soul need to be taken care of so you will have extra energy to take care of others and all the details. If you are not calm and centered, there is little chance your dream will flourish. Along the path to your dream, take care of yourself and you will deliver into this world your heart's desire.

Money Is Rarely the Real Obstacle

There's one more limiting belief worth discussing—and this one is perhaps the most common. In these difficult economic times, the limiting belief I hear expressed most often is, "I don't have the finances to handle it." I ask, "How much do you need?"

The most common answer is, "I don't know, but I know I don't have enough."

You might be thinking, "Wait a minute—my bank balance is not a belief; it's a reality!" Sometimes not having enough is a reality, but sometimes it's a limiting belief, and usually there are creative alternatives for handling this issue. Frequently, however, the very people who express reservations based on their finances are the ones who can't afford to stay where they are. From an economic perspective, they would benefit from making a change.

Caroll heard me speak one day and was inspired to attend a workshop I was leading. "I'd love to come," she said, "but there's no way I can afford it." As the words came out of her mouth, her expression changed.

"I am so sick of hearing myself tell that same old story!" she said, shaking her head. "I am unwilling to continue to let money be what stops me from having what I want. Here's my credit card for the deposit. I will find a way to make this happen."

When she got home, she posted my flyer and her intention in plain sight. In big letters she wrote: I will easily attend Dream University®.

The next day, she opened her mail and found one of her investments was not doing well. She decided to sell it to pay off her credit card debt. She called me immediately.

"It's amazing! I paid off all my debt and have exactly enough money to fully cover both my tuition and travel expenses. This experience changed the way I look at life. I will no longer kill off my dreams just because I don't know how they will occur. I'll commit to what I want and find a way to make it happen."

Caroll came to the workshop, and over and over she kept noticing when she said "no," where her limiting beliefs were having her play it safe, and how she would try to kill off any new possibilities. After a week of this, we rewired her internal circuitry.

Caroll now knows and teaches that it's rarely money that stops us. She has become one of my most successful Certified Dream Coaches® with a thriving practice, working with exactly the clientele she wants and on her terms. There is true power in acting on what you really want. She recently told me, she has never been happier; she feels totally free and is facing unlimited horizons for her career and personal life. There is nothing like releasing the burden of carrying around a big limiting belief to free you to find your true power and Essence, and even some unexpected sources of funding.

Keep in mind there are countless ways to finance a dream or good idea. You can barter or trade services, ask people to invest in you, and find a myriad of other alternatives. But remember, if you don't believe in your dream, no one else will either.

CHAPTER 9

Commit To Your Dreamer

*I can't imagine a person becoming a success
who doesn't give this game of life everything he's got.*

—Walter Cronkite

"It is possible." Those three words are at the core of having your dream come true. If you have read this far in the book and you confess that you still don't believe you can have your dream, turn back to the previous chapter and confront and handle your negative beliefs before you go on. You can't make your dream come true if you don't believe it's possible. And only when you believe it's possible are you ready to take the life-changing step I'll be teaching in this chapter: committing to your Dreamer.

Your Dreamer is the other voice inside your head—the one that says, "yes!" and gets excited when you consider new possibilities for your life. Your Dreamer is not burdened by your fears, doubts, and limiting beliefs. It's the part of you that knows anything is possible. When you get in touch with that part of yourself and make a commitment to pledge your allegiance to your Dreamer rather than to your Doubter, your life will change faster than you can imagine.

I often find myself acting as that believer for others. If you don't believe in yourself, it's hard for others to as well. A big part of my job is getting others to believe in themselves. If we had to have evidence to believe in everything, half the things that exist in the world today would never have come to be.

If you're having trouble getting in touch with your Dreamer, go back to your purpose statement and connect with your passion. Read your dream description aloud. Then try this simple sentence-completion exercise to bring out the voice of your Dreamer.

Speaking aloud or writing in your Dream Book, complete the following sentences in the voice of your Dreamer:

- The dream I have for (your name) is _____. . . .

- If I were in charge of (your name)'s life I would_____. . . .

- My purpose in (your name)'s life is_____. . . .

- (Your name) can have more access to me by_____. . . .

How does that feel? The voice of your Dreamer is confident, passionate, and reassuring. And here's the secret to getting more of that in your life: you have to commit to the Dreamer.

I sometimes refer to "commitment" as the "C" word, because a lot of people think of it as if it were an obscenity. Perhaps they view commitment as synonymous with being trapped, or it makes them feel locked in.

When I speak of commitment, I mean a covenant with yourself and for yourself; committing to something you want, to having your dream come true, to moving forward. Commitment is hardly a dirty word; on the contrary, it's a powerful experience. Many of the people I coach find that once they get to the commitment stage, dramatic things happen.

A commitment is not just a feeling or an idea—it's a stake in the ground. It's something that demonstrates your allegiance to your Dreamer rather than your Doubter. Ask yourself what kind of commitment you are willing to make to achieve your dream. The answer might surprise you.

I worked with one couple, Tim and Sally Carter, who owned a successful computer store in a fancy shopping center. Like many people, their dream was to have financial freedom while having the time to enjoy each other. When I asked them during a session what was working against that dream, Tim said, "Maintaining our current business." Both he and Sally looked startled at the words that had come out of his mouth. Neither of them had realized it until that moment, but the massive overhead in their upscale setting was eroding their profits, and the retail nature of their establishment meant they were always on-call when the store was open. They needed more flexibility, and they now recognized in order to have that flexibility, they would have to close the store and transition into a new business. What surprised them was they were both willing to do it, despite the risks.

Setting a date for this sale made their commitment tangible. And the Carters began to see the possibilities as soon as they put their stake in the ground. First, they realized they could have a whole new consulting business serving clients with whom they had done business before. Second, they determined their retail business could be sold to someone who would continue to serve their previous customers. Third, the new owner agreed to refer retail customers who needed consultation about purchases made at the store. In other words, they took their dream to a new level by evolving a new relationship. Within three months they had phased out of their retail operation and created a new business that gave them greater flexibility and the opportunity to be in closer partnership with each other. And rather than simply separating themselves from their previous business, they found a way to make a profitable connection for their new business. But none of these possibilities would have appeared had they not been willing to make that initial commitment to their dream, despite the risks.

Once you are committed to making your dream come true, everything seems to move faster, and you will find that you seem to know with greater certainty how you need to proceed. Your next step becomes evident, as does the step after that. Nevertheless there are some common attitudes and beliefs that stop people from making a commitment to themselves:

- "It's going to force my hand."

- "I'll be stuck with it and won't be able to change direction later."

- "It might be the wrong move and if I keep my options open something better might show up."

- "I might look silly."

- "It will take longer for me to get there than I care to invest."

- "I might not be able to do what I say."

- "I might not be able to follow through."

- "What if I fail?"

You can deal with these beliefs in the same way you dealt with other limiting beliefs in chapter eight: you can redefine commitment as something positive, a tool that can be used to propel you toward having your dream, which is exactly what it is. Commitment is a much more powerful way of living than waiting around and hoping, or worse, never doing anything to make your dreams happen. Consider these new beliefs you might adopt about commitment:

- "It's going to open up new possibilities."

- "I choose it. Life is full of choices."

- "It might be a good move, and by staying committed other good things will show up."

- "It won't take long for me to get there."

- "I do exactly what I say."

- "I will be able to follow through."

- "I intend to succeed."

The Sliding Glass Door

One of my favorite exercises for learning to live in your commitment is called "The Sliding Glass Door." Here's how it works.

Remove yourself from outside distractions by putting yourself someplace where you won't be disturbed. Relax. Take a few deep breaths. This exercise is completely about you, about stepping into your commitment.

Imagine that you're standing with your nose pressed against a glass door, so close to it that your breath is steaming up the glass. As you wipe away the steam, you see a beautiful place on the other side of the glass. Rainbows, waterfalls, meadows, animals—your dream world, however you imagine it at its most beautiful.

Feel your feet standing on the floor on your side of the glass door. The glass door is like that line you drew in your Dream Book, and you're standing in the section marked "Where I Am Now." All around you is your current life, with everything that's happening right now, including your attitudes and beliefs. Looking through the glass door, you can see the beauty on the other side. You will now have the opportunity to find out if the other side is a place you want to be.

Grasp the handle and slide the door open. A gentle, warm breeze comes wafting in, and there's a delicious smell in the air. You feel warm and welcomed.

As you gaze around, you see everything you want, everything that's in your dream, everything you're committed to having. Your family is there, too, your friends, your dream house, your dream life. All the elements of your dream are there, on the other side of the door.

Notice where you are and where you want to be. All you need to do to get to the other side is make the commitment and step through.

Ask yourself, "Is this what I want? Will I commit to this?" If the answer is "yes," lift your foot and step across.

Now you're on the other side, living in a land of possibilities. Here's where all your dreams can come true. Don't worry if you don't have it all figured out. Just trust: now that you're standing in your commitment, you're standing in your dream.

Of course, you might decide not to commit and step through the now open door. That's fine. Be clear that this side of the glass door is where you choose to be right now. Ask yourself why, and if you discover a limiting belief, you might decide to go back to chapter eight and transform it into an empowering one. Your dream will always be there on the other side of the sliding glass door. When you are ready, reach out, slide it open, and step through.

If you're hesitating, you can also choose to suspend your negative attitude and say, "I'll believe it for a while and give it a shot." However, I recommend you walk through that door and close it behind you— that's where you'll discover the power of commitment. Be committed to having your dream come true, be willing to have it be possible, allow your attitudes and beliefs to support you, and stop holding onto some outdated negative opinion. Step through; that's where the surprises will happen. Being open to possibility means you are open to hope, and hope invites us to say "yes" to life. From here there are many opportunities to handle all of your concerns and help move you to the next step.

Integrity: The Key to Manifestation

One of the most common reasons people hesitate to commit is the fear they won't follow through. And you know what? The most common reason people fail to follow through on their stated intentions is because they don't add the ingredient of integrity.

Survey big dreamers on the value they most respect and usually at the top of the list is integrity. If you are committed to living a life of joy, ease, and abundance, a life filled with love, generosity, and contribution, integrity is a must. But it always surprises me how many people guide others in setting intentions and making commitments but leave out this critical element.

Without integrity, intention is just a nice idea. Intention is the rudder that sets the course and steers your life, but integrity is what makes it solid and stick. Align your life with your intentions by keeping your promises to yourself and others. Too often, people will say they want something or they intend to do something, and then they just do something else. Or worse still, they do nothing. That is what activates the Doubter, and solidifies all of its limiting beliefs and attitudes.

Remember how I identified mistrust as one of the three categories of limiting beliefs? One of the most powerful forms of mistrust is mistrust of ourselves. When we lie to ourselves and don't follow through on our commitments, we learn not to trust ourselves. So in order to rebuild self-trust and be able to experience the power of commitment, it's essential that you break these unhealthy habits and start to build integrity. In other words, do what you say you're going to do, actually be as good as your word, walk your talk.

Right now, your dream doesn't exist in reality. It begins to take on life as you envision it and speak about it. When you commit, a new dynamic will start to show up, bringing opportunities you didn't know were possible. Be especially careful at this point to avoid being stopped by limiting beliefs and attitudes; sometimes in the commitment phase, self-sabotage can sneak up on you when you're least expecting it. If you're not responsible about following through on your commitment, the process will start to unravel and you will undermine yourself and your dream.

When I was unexpectedly invited to take my dream holiday in Greece, I respectfully dismissed the voice of my Doubter and bought my ticket. That was my stake in the ground—now I was committed. So why, when a client called to offer me a great speaking gig that would occur right smack in the middle of that holiday, did I accept the job, volunteering to cut my vacation time in half? That evening I noticed I was grumpy with the people I love and became suspicious that something was going on, something that I was not aware of. Then it hit me. I was selling out on my own dream.

The next day I called my client back and apologized, telling her I would not be able to speak at her event. "Why?" she had to ask. I took a deep breath, and for a moment, was concerned about what she would think of me. "I'm going to Greece to pursue a long overdue dream. I'm sorry."

"Why would you be sorry? I'm just sorry I'm not going with you. We'll try to schedule you to speak at our conference next year," she said.

These sabotaging patterns can be subtle and sneaky. For example, you might be committed to doing something even though you're worried about not having the time or money to do it. Don't stop acting because of your concern—remind yourself that money is rarely the obstacle you think it is. By acting on your commitment, you open up opportunities—perhaps some new resource that will make the whole thing feasible. If you are willing to make the commitment down to the marrow in your bones, amazing things will happen in your life, including the fact that wonderful people will emerge to help you. This is not about being flaky or irresponsible. Show up fully for what you want, even if it takes you into foreign territory.

Agreements

Integrity means keeping your agreements—with other people and with yourself, perhaps especially with yourself. Our ability to make and keep agreements with ourselves and others is one of the key ways to build trust. The more you keep your agreements, the more you can trust yourself, and the more others will trust you, too. But keeping agreements with ourselves is hard. That's why coaching has become a multi-billion-dollar industry: when we tell someone else what we're going to do it increases the likelihood we'll do it.

Keeping agreements doesn't mean forcing yourself to do things you don't want to do. But it might mean you need to stop saying you're going to do things if you're not going to follow through. For example, if you say you are going to go to the gym three times this week, last week, and next week, but never go, stop saying it and take it off your list. Remember what I said about lingering dreams? If you have a dream, goal, or task that remains on your to-do list, year in and out, either *do it or dump it*. Stop suffering by saying you are going to do things you don't do and then feeling guilty about it. Replace them with new dreams and projects that you intend to accomplish. Say what you mean and mean what you say.

Perhaps the most significant agreement you can keep is to live on purpose. Spending most of your time putting out fires or solving problems, filling your days with things that don't nurture you at a soul level, is out of integrity. Conversely, when you are in touch with your gifts, every conversation counts, every encounter is a chance to touch or serve another, and every moment is rich and meaningful. You will feel whole, which is what integrity really means.

The Power of Personal Practices

Keeping agreements isn't easy, especially when you're trying to change deeply entrenched patterns of belief or behavior or lifelong habits. While we are often aware of our shortcomings, and have good intentions for changing them, we might not know what to do about them. If you are tired of getting stuck in that same old place, a personal practice can make it easier to commit to making a shift.

Personal practices are simply agreements you make with yourself to do something particular each day, each week, or each time you catch yourself acting out of the old behavior. A practice is something you do on an ongoing basis. Any time there is a habit you want to change or a new skill you want to develop, personal practices are an important tool. For example, if your dream is to live a life of ease and creativity, and you are trying to change a behavior pattern of overworking and being stressed, you might choose to create a personal practice of meditating for twenty minutes each day. Following through on this commitment by doing that tangible practice will anchor you in your intention to create more time and space for yourself. And it will move you closer to your dream—studies have proven that meditation reduces stress and many people report that it opens up their creative faculties.

An artist I knew complained she never had time to paint. We both saw that although she could juggle many things at once, important things rarely got completed. When she told me her dream was to create enough paintings to have her own show, I offered her this personal practice:

"For one hour each day, complete what you are doing before you move on to something else. That means, if you are checking email and the phone rings, let it roll into voice mail."

She was outraged. "This is going to stifle my creativity."

I calmly replied, "A little structure allows for more creativity."

"Alright, I'll try it for a week," she reluctantly said.

We agreed that each day she would give me an update via voice mail. Here's the synopsis:

Day 1: "I hate this," her curt message screeched.

Day 2: "This is the wrong practice for me."

Day 3: "I lasted thirty minutes and made some progress."

Day 4: "I am wondering why I don't make my needs a priority. I cried. I think we're onto something."

Day 5: "This is amazing. I feel lighter and got so much done."

Day 6: "I'm going to continue this for another week."

Her second week was so streamlined she had time left over to organize her forgotten studio. By week three she was painting again. After three months she had completed more art than she had for the entire previous year. With newfound clarity, self-confidence, and self-worth, her art was also selling again. Now, her assistant is managing her office allowing her to happily be where she belongs, in her studio. All of this came about from the simple practice of focusing one hour a day.

To experience the power of personal practices, first identify where you get stuck or how you sabotage your dreams. What would you like to change or develop? What could you do differently and how many times a day or a week will you do it? Practice being the person you dream of being and soon it will become automatic and part of you. And be sure to celebrate your newly acquired skill.

You might want to develop a personal practice to overcome a particular habit—like negative self-talk, overcommitting, or procrastination. For these kinds of habits, a powerful way to practice is to choose something you will do every time you catch yourself in the act of doing the old behavior. It could be as simple as this: every time you become aware that you're caught in the pattern, press an internal pause button. Then do something different. For example, let's say you have a habit of negative self-talk, and you're walking down the street one morning and catch a glimpse of yourself in a window, "You look terrible!" says the voice in your head. Press pause as soon as you realize what's happening. Stop the train of negative commentary and, instead, tell yourself a new story. Say something kind to yourself. Remind yourself of your best, most lovable qualities. Don't let yourself be hijacked by your Doubter or your limiting beliefs.

Perhaps you recognize that you tend to sabotage your dreams by not taking care of yourself. You work so hard that you burn yourself out, and then you get sick and fail to follow through on your agreements. In this case, you might consider personal practices like committing to get a massage once a week, going to bed at a certain time each night, or turning off your cell phone once you get home. Often, personal practices require saying "no" to old habits in order to make way for new ones—something we'll talk more about in the next chapter.

In any area of your life where you recognize a limiting pattern of self-sabotage, design a personal practice. It will strengthen your commitment, deepen your self-trust, and make you a bigger dreamer and a better person.

Commitment Releases Creativity

Again, does any of this mean you're guaranteed not to fail? Of course not. Failure is a part of life, and often it can be the source of our greatest lessons. But what I love about dreams is precisely the fact that they are not about promises, guarantees, and assurances. They are about things that matter enough to you that you're willing to put a stake in the ground and commit to them anyway.

When you've made a commitment to your Dreamer, you will have a different perspective on your dream than you did when you were wondering if it would ever happen. Maybe you once thought you didn't have the time or money to go after that new piece of business you want; now that you're committed to doing it and you've dealt with all of your negative attitudes and beliefs, you might see the logic of freeing time or resources by giving up something that doesn't interest you anymore.

Your new outlook, that it makes sense to give up something that no longer has value to you, is a direct result of your commitment to being where you want to be, not where you are. Refocusing on your life's purpose (who you are and what turns you on) will assist you in deciding when to give up or walk away from something. In the following chapter, I'll be teaching you a powerful exercise for saying "no more" to those things that no longer serve your purpose. You'll notice a lighter, freer feeling as you let go of the old and create room to embrace the new.

CHAPTER 10
Make Space for Your Dream

Our real work is heart work and soul work.

—Matthew Fox

Four of my favorite words for making dreams come true are: "No more. Now what?" When you say "no more" to things that no longer support your dreams, you make space to ask, "Now what?" and welcome new opportunities into your life.

It's difficult to create your future now when you feel overburdened, overwhelmed, and overcommitted. When you are full to the brim it's hard to be open to new creativity. When asked to do something, do you open a jam-packed calendar to squeeze one more thing into an already over-scheduled life? As we saw in the last chapter, when you commit to your dream, you're likely to begin to recognize some of the things in your life that are taking up too much space. In this chapter, I'll be sharing the powerful practice of saying "no more" to those things, and also teaching you how to bring completion to areas of your life where unfinished business is draining your dreams and sapping your energy.

The ability to stop and take a breath (which includes exhaling) is what makes space for new ideas and dreams. I call this the art of emptying. It's also important not to have every hour of every day scheduled, so that you can allow for some of the serendipity of life. Can you be available if someone calls last minute and wants to have a cup of coffee with you or an amazing opportunity opens up? For example, on a recent trip abroad, I was with a friend and he pointed out an international spiritual center. I mentioned I'd been wanting to meet the founder, Karen Berg, who in fact lives near me in Beverly Hills, but had never had the opportunity. My friend pulled out his phone and hit a speed dial button—it turned out he knew her and she was in town that day. "Bring her over now!" she told him. So I spent a wonderful afternoon dreamstorming with Karen, and we came up with an idea for a special event we want to create in Los Angeles when we are both back in town. If my life had been scheduled with back-to-back meetings, that never would have happened.

As you deepen your ability to listen to your Dreamer, you will learn how to make more space in your life. Your senses become more acute, you develop a greater sensitivity to people and things around you, and you learn to recognize what's true and what's not for you. You recognize false securities, illusions, and what no longer serves you. And you learn to let go of people, ideas, and things that don't work.

When your kids need you or you are under deadline at work, you don't always have a choice. But when offered a choice, if you are invited to do something you don't have to do or don't want to do, consider saying, "No, thank you."

Practice emptying yourself out and clearing the clutter of your mind and life. If you want to achieve your dreams, you need to create space for them, not just in your closets or your office, but in yourself. Make room in your life for your dreams.

No More. Now What?

Is it time to give up something you have outgrown? Are you ready to quit something that is no longer true for you and no longer nurtures or fulfills you? What activities or responsibilities in your life could you say "no more" to?

Make a list of all the habits, responsibilities, and even relationships you find yourself complaining about, that are sucking the life out of you, no longer feel true to who you are, and are out of integrity with your heart and soul. Your list might include a habit that distracts you from your purpose, a group you're participating in that you no longer feel aligned with, or a bad behavior that gets you in trouble. It might even be a relationship that is one-sided, with someone who takes you for granted.

As you say, "no more" to what's no longer true for you, to those activities and even relationships that are not aligned with how you want to live your life, you make room to ask, "Now what?" With newfound friends, energy, and time, what would you say yes to? What would you say "more" to? What dreams would you now schedule into your life? Saying "no more, now what?" makes space for two more of my favorite words: "what else?" What else would bring you more joy and fulfillment, what else would bring you more passion and energy, what else would have you feeling aligned with your purpose?

With a little breathing space, you can add things to your life that matter to you; that make you happy and are aligned with your purpose.

One client of mine, Andy, shared a simple but powerful example. His dreams included living a happier, healthier life and being more connected to his family. So he said, "No more TV after dinner!"

"Why?" I asked him. "What's the cost?" It's important to know why you're saying "no more" to something and frame the answer in terms of the cost to your life. For most of us, it's not enough to just vaguely think something isn't good for us—we need to recognize its consequences and connect them to something we care about.

Andy had a clear answer: "I'm getting lazy and sloppy; I'm withdrawing from my family and becoming less sociable."

"Okay," I said. "Let's do it! No more TV after dinner. Now what?"

When I next saw him, three months later, I could already see the answer. He looked healthier, happier, and more alert. I asked him to tell me his "now what;" to tell me what became possible with the new space he'd created each evening.

"That simple decision has changed my life!" he declared. Without the television to suck away his time and attention, he started taking walks with his family after dinner. As a result, he got healthier and closer to his wife and his kids. During those walks, he found time to talk to them about their dreams and support them in making similar choices.

Here's a "No more. Now what?" that's been important for me: "No more chocolate for breakfast!"

You might laugh, but that bad habit actually had a serious cost. It set me up for cravings all day long. My taste buds became numb and I lost interest in healthy, delicious food. I gained weight and suffered from headaches.

So I said, "No more chocolate for breakfast." Now what? I jump out of bed in the morning feeling full of vitality. I eat a healthy breakfast so I feel ready for the day. I love my body and wear cuter outfits; I feel alive and energized; I'm writing a new book and pursuing many other projects that express my dreams—all because I said, "No more chocolate for breakfast."

After you make the decision to say "no more" to something, it's important to remember the power of personal practices (see chapter nine). Often, you will need to put a practice in place in order to keep that agreement with yourself and make your "no more" stick.

Ask yourself, what could you say "no more" to today? Then ask yourself *why*—what's the cost of that activity, responsibility, or relationship? How does it affect your dreams? And what might become possible if it was no longer part of your life?

Sometimes, the thing you say "no more" to might be something that seems very positive. You might not even be sure what the cost is—perhaps you just have a sense that it's time to move on and make space for something else. After I trained and certified my thousandth Dream Coach®, I had an intuition that this role was no longer mine. My friends and colleagues thought this was crazy. "It's incredibly lucrative!" they reminded me. "It's one of your most successful programs." But I knew there was a bigger vision that wanted to come in and I needed to make space in my life by saying no to something. As

I was preparing for the last Dream Coach® Certification event, I got the idea that I should film the entire thing. Years later, it was turned into a very successful online coach certification program, and I had time on my hands for new possibilities. Even though it didn't seem logical at the time, it was saying "no more" to training coaches that actually opened the door for me to create The Meaning Institute, my year-long in-depth transformational program, which I'll be sharing more about in chapter fifteen.

Incompletions

Sometimes saying "no more" is as simple as turning off the television or reaching for an apple instead of chocolate. But there might be other things in your life that sap your energy and attention and are not so easy to just be done with. If something in your life is incomplete, you might need to take action to complete or resolve it before you can let it go. For example, there might be a project you've been avoiding and left half-done, or a close relationship that has gotten stuck in disagreement. How do you know if something is incomplete? It bugs you and usurps your energy. Ask yourself if the matter is settled. Do you think about it or worry about it? Is this impacting other areas of your life? When we are complete with something, often we don't even think about it. There is no agitation or energy wasted. If you think of something and you feel little or no internal reaction, then you're probably complete with that thing.

Wherever you are incomplete, especially with people, sooner or later it will show up. You might be abrupt or judgmental about something someone says or does and it might have little to do with them. If there is someone with whom you are incomplete or someone to whom you have not said something that you need to say, it will likely get in your way again and again, often with different people. Practice "being complete" in all of your relationships. This includes moms, dads, brothers, sisters, spouses, children, friends, lovers, bosses, and colleagues.

Only you can define if something is incomplete or not. You set the standard here. Leave no skeletons gathering cobwebs in your closets. When you clean up your past by completing things, you have so much more energy and clarity to focus on your dreams and plan your future.

At different times in our lives, many of us have been the victim of a pile-up of incompletions. One man I know didn't pay his taxes for two years. The IRS put a lien on his assets, so he looked like a bad credit risk. He couldn't buy a house or rent an apartment. Eventually he lost his credit cards. He was caught in a downward spiral that also undermined his confidence and self-esteem. Another woman I know let her parking tickets pile high. She never got around to paying them. She became afraid of driving her car because she might get towed. Concerned about driving to work, she eventually lost her job. A small detail led to a bigger concern, which led to an even bigger problem.

The three big areas to check for incompletions are health, money, and relationships. But you could also be tying yourself down with physical clutter and mess. It's difficult to focus on creating and dreaming when you have parking tickets that are overdue or garbage all over your apartment.

When you have clothes or shoes all around the house, dishes piled in the sink or a buried desk, you might be out of sorts. We don't need to be obsessive about this. We just want to recognize signs. When life is overly cluttered, often so are we. Learn to see what's in your space. Recognize where you're sluggish or sloppy and clean it up.

My friend Nancy was invited to relocate to Paris but couldn't move until she sold her home. She confided there was one room in the house that she jokingly referred to as the "black hole," because it was piled high with countless incomplete items. I suggested that it might be a powerful practice for her to complete those tasks, and perhaps it would prove effective in accelerating her dream. Following my advice, Nancy ventured into her "black hole" and came out with a list of close to one hundred items to do, including returning borrowed books, writing overdue letters, even mailing back an inexpensive bracelet she had taken from her neighborhood drug store when she was a teenager. It took some time and effort initially, but with each item she handled, Nancy felt lighter and freer. And within a few weeks of completing her list, she easily sold her house and made the big move. The view from her new kitchen window includes the Eiffel Tower, and there are no black holes in her sunny apartment.

I have a simple and powerful process for exploring what's incomplete in your life. Don't be deceived by its apparent simplicity because, if undertaken fully, it might be one of the most profound things you ever do. And once you clean house there is a big payoff. You will experience tremendous peace of mind with ample room for new dreams.

Here are the three simple steps:

1. Ask yourself what's incomplete and write it down, including the name if it involves a person.
2. Ask yourself what you need to do to complete this.
3. Complete what's incomplete.

Here are some areas where you can apply this process:

Body. How's your health? When is the last time you had a physical or had your blood pressure checked? Do you have nagging symptoms you've been avoiding getting checked out?

Mind. Are you relaxed or stressed? How do you sleep at night? Do you meditate or quiet your mind? Do you have a psychological or spiritual path for growth? Is it working for you? Have you considered therapy or retreats?

Home. Is your physical space cluttered? Are there things about it that bother you and prevent you from focusing on what matters?

Car. Do you have one, need one, or want one? Do you want to get rid of it? Do you get regular maintenance and oil changes? Is your insurance current? Does your car have dents and dings? Does that bother you? How do you feel driving it? How about parking tickets or moving violations? Are you legal and safe?

Work. How do you feel about what you do? Are there issues at work you've been avoiding dealing with or projects you haven't finished that are long overdue? Are there things you're hiding from your boss or co-workers?

Finance. How's your debt? Are you current on your finance payments? Do you have an IRA or retirement fund? Do you save money regularly? Do you spend more than you earn? How do you feel about your financial position? How are you at managing your money? Do you have someone to help you? Do you find yourself avoiding the topic and being unconscious of your spending because it all feels unmanageable? Are you charging enough for your services or making an appropriate salary? (We'll be talking more about this in chapter thirteen.)

People. Survey all your relationships. Look at work, home, friends, family, people from your present and your past. Do you have borrowed items to return, calls to make, letters to write, apologies to offer? Are you overdue with a wedding gift or a belated birthday card? Is there anyone you are hiding from? Is there an unfinished conversation, an unresolved conflict, or a request you need to make? Is there someone who has wronged you in past that you need to confront or to forgive? Is there someone you have hurt, from whom you need to seek forgiveness? Are you willing to initiate it at this time? What do you need to do to heal or complete your relationships?

My invitation to you today is to just make the list and try to complete *one* item. Completions might include writing a letter, making a phone call, or communicating gratitude, appreciation, or forgiveness to a loved one. Some completions might involve an apology. Sometimes you can create a ritual to bring closure to the past. With some, you might just declare that it's over. With some, you might not know. Decide which item on your list you intend to accomplish today or this week. Eventually, I recommend doing them all. But try to do so from a place of grace rather than from a place of wanting to control everything. Having a sense of humor; maintaining a certain amount of lightness is also very useful. What you are going for is a feeling of completion and ease (if you find yourself obsessing and feeling tense, you know something needs adjusting). Life is easier and flows better when it's intact, when you are whole. It's just that simple.

This process is so powerful, you can use it to get completion with anything in your life—no matter how big. You can even get complete with someone who has died. I know a woman who wanted an intimate relationship, but her fear of loss kept her from committing to anyone new because she had had a dear friend die at a young age from AIDS.

She missed him terribly and had never felt complete with his death, so she decided to go to his grave site and have a conversation with him.

She bought flowers and bubbles to blow—something he had loved. But when she got there, she was so surprised to hear what came out of her mouth. She was filled with rage. She had planned on having a lifelong friendship with this person and now he was gone. After two hours of yelling, crying, laughing, and blowing bubbles, she was finally able to put it to rest. Her friend lives on in her heart and she doesn't have such an intense reaction when she hears the sad news of someone else with AIDS or any other illness. A few weeks later, she met someone wonderful, and fell head-over-heels in love.

The secret to a life of ease is to clean up your messes and then, once again, design a personal practice or system that doesn't allow them to recur. Complete what you start, when you start it, even if it's to decide not to do it anymore. Keep your mind relaxed and available for the things that matter to you. You will most likely find this approach to be life-changing.

As we become more well-rounded, which comes from doing our personal work, the quality of people and the level of integrity by which we live our lives will increase.

The Big Payoff

The sense of accomplishment you will feel as you clear off your list will amaze you. This is not the same process as simply checking things off a laundry list. You are in the process of cleaning up your entire life and freeing yourself from the weight of the unresolved past.

The big payoff here comes back to integrity. Integrity is defined as the quality of being complete, whole, and unbroken, and being sound, honest, and sincere. When we are whole, people can count on us and we can count on ourselves. Practicing integrity is one of the greatest ways to build self-confidence and self-trust.

When you're not looking over your shoulder, at all the incompletions in your life, you can be focused on moving ahead. When you are not hiding skeletons in your closet, you can be open and take risks. And when you are not cleaning up messes from the past, you are free to create and design big, new, wonderful dreams for the future. When your energy isn't diffused or wasted in a fixing or fretting mode, you are available to play. People start to see that they can count on you. Your word becomes extremely valuable. Keeping your word is how you show others that you are serious about your intention. Keeping your word is how you show yourself that you are accountable. You demonstrate to yourself that your word is powerful because you honor what you say.

Living with integrity in this way opens the door for a simple but profound concept that I call everyday enlightenment. It basically means that every day you spend more time connected to your dreams, doing things you truly love and are meaningful to you. It also means you spend less time in the dark, being hijacked by your own and other people's fears and doubts, forgetting who you are, or doing things that are unkind or not thoughtful. The secret to living a joyful, fulfilling life is doing more of what you love every day. And of course, in order to do that, you need to quit or eliminate the things that take you away from your purpose and dreams.

The more your life is in order, the faster and easier your ability to manifest will become. You'll find that almost as soon as you say what you want or ask for what you need, it shows up. When your home, business, and relationships are solid and working, your integrity is fully intact. Miraculously, you will find that by doing less, you can have more. It will require some courage, but trust me, it works. I have helped thousands of people take control of their lives, so I know you can take control of yours, too. Living a more conscious life every single day doesn't require a lot of effort or struggle or compromise or loss. It simply requires your desire, willingness, and, of course, commitment.

PART THREE

ACT *on Your Dream*

CHAPTER 11
Project Your Dream

Cherish your visions and your dreams, as they are the children of your soul, the blueprints of your ultimate achievements.

—Napoleon Hill

A dear friend once told me that turning dreams into projects is a way to project yourself into the future. I loved this because it reminded me that "project," like "dream," is both a noun and a verb. Many of us, when we see the word "project," think first of the noun and associate it with homework assignments or work deadlines. In this chapter, I'll be encouraging you to leave those negative associations aside and remember that projects *project* your dreams into the future. They are the bridge between where you are and where you want to be. Dreams—especially big ones—die when they're just left on a list. When you turn your dream into a project with specific, measurable results, break it down into steps, and create strategies for accomplishing them, the action of doing so will make your dream begin to exist in your life, not just in your head or on paper.

Possibility starts to feel more like probability when you move forward from dreams to projects. As you start to involve yourself in the specific results, the dream will become animated and take on credibility. Everything up to this point—all the exercises, visualizations, writings—have been a projection of what you want to have. Now we will transform it all into projects and strategies.

Creating Projects

I recommend creating projects that can easily be accomplished within one month or less. One month is a short enough time for you to stay passionate and engaged, but a long enough time for you to see results. You must see real results to stay motivated. Here are the criteria I use when creating projects. They should:

1. Move you forward on your dream
2. Be something you're passionate about
3. Be specific and measurable
4. Be something you can easily accomplish within one month

Remember that everything comes from purpose. Standing in your purpose, ask, with respect to the area of life you have selected to work on, "What dream do I have that I can turn into an exciting project?" Make sure the project fits the criteria above. Then look for what needs to be added to your project to get it scheduled into your life—a date, a person, or a contact number.

Here are some sample dreams and projects from people who participated in The Meaning Institute:

Dream: Climb Mt. Kilimanjaro

Project: Within one month, hire a trainer to map out our plan.

Name: Melanie Bragg, J.D., Author of *Crosstown Park*

Dream: Be a master at healing the world.

Project: Within one month, reach out to each of my patients with my heart, and begin healing one soul at a time.

Name: Dr. Alan Chong, The Spine Coach

Dream: To create leaders whose teams and communities will make the leap of faith to create, innovate and achieve exciting new heights.

Project: Within one month, create the outline of the Inspired Leaders Passion Adventure Series.

Name: Lori Cammerota, CEO, Opendoorzstrategy.com

Dream: To awaken millions who fear dementia and empower them to recognize the early signs and avoid the danger.

Project: Within one month, complete my book.

Name: Dorothy Kuhn, *The Mender of Memory*

Dream: To serve as a catalyst to awaken children and the "inner children" of adults to their divine gifts and the missions of their heroic hearts.

Project: Within one month, conduct twenty-five "Soul Purpose" readings for children and adults.

Name: Hal Price, Heroic Heart Specialist

Dream: To make an impact on as many people as I can across the world to not be judgmental.

Project: Within one month, launch my "Everyone Deserves to Be Heard" movement by securing a live speaking gig on this topic.

Name: Beverly Bergman, The Big Vision Catalyst

Dream: To guide others from pain to peace and enable them to "in-joy" the life they were meant to live.

Project: Within one month, to get five new clients in order to provide income for my wife and I to attend The Meaning Institute together.

Name: Anthony Diaz, The Peace Maker

Dream: To support the dreams of mission-driven entrepreneurs by connecting them to the money needed to complete their missions.

Project: Within one month, to connect ten entrepreneurs with their money through my program.

Name: Cynthia Stott, Creator, The Divine Money Messages

Dream: For my leadership program to be integrated in all schools; for all children to know they are worthy, valuable, and that their unique gifts and talents matter.

Project: Within one month I will produce an inspiring event for fifty kids and adults.

Name: Anna Herbert, Founder, Playground of Dreams

Some projects are easy; you merely have to schedule them into your calendar. Others are complicated, and require a well-thought-out plan to get there. And remember, a project has to be specific, but it can deal with any aspect of your life. Don't make the mistake of thinking projects only apply to your professional life. For instance, if your dream is to travel the world, your first project might be to plan to go on a vacation this year. That certainly moves you forward on your dream and, therefore, will ignite your passion. You can set yourself a measurable, specific goal of choosing the location and booking the trip within one month.

If your dream is to spend more time with your family, you might create a project to renegotiate your work hours with your team at the office, handing over some specific responsibilities and empowering others so that you can work from home one day a week, or reduce your hours. This puts you in action toward the dream you are passionate about, it has clear, measurable results, and it's achievable within one month.

Some dreams will require only one project; others might include multiple projects. Perhaps your dream is to build a business based on your purpose. In that case, you'll have to create numerous projects—a project to write a business plan, another project to transition out of your former job, and another project to find a business partner or a venture capital firm that's interested in funding your dream. Each of these projects is a definable goal that moves you toward your dream and can be accomplished within one month. They can then be further broken down into steps, as we'll see later in this chapter.

Looking Back at This Year

One helpful exercise for identifying projects that will help you achieve your dream is the Looking Back exercise. Project yourself out in your mind's eye to a point one year from today. On that day, you are standing in your life's purpose, already living the dream you have deliberately chosen, having removed all the limiting beliefs and obstacles.

Now you will look back from that point and write out how the last year was for you. You might ask yourself:

- What were you passionate about?

- Where did your achievements take place?

- Who else was involved?

- What funds became available?

- How did you spend the extra money that came your way?

- How did others respond?

- How did you feel as you passed certain milestones?

- How did going down one path take you to another?

- Whom did you meet this year that you always wanted to meet?

- How did you spend your exotic vacation?

- How did you look and feel?

- How was the last year for you, now that you made your dream come true?

- Looking back, what was at least one critical decision you made today that put you on the path or trajectory to accomplish this dream this year?

This last question is key. For example, to accomplish transforming my year and ultimately my life, I decided to trust life and myself on a much deeper level. That one choice was a game-changer for me, helping me take bigger risks, partner with new people, travel to new destinations, and say yes much more deliberately to what life was offering to me.

Be specific when you're looking back. State your accomplishments during the last year—they will give you the clues to the steps between now and your dream, steps that can be turned into projects. Draw the complete picture for yourself, leaving out none of the details. Remember, you stepped through the Sliding Glass Door.

Through projecting yourself into the future to look back at the past, you can develop a game plan that is based upon where you want to be, rather than where you are. This is a powerful technique for designing projects and also for creating strategies, which we'll discuss in the next chapter.

Let more and more come to you as you're writing; you'll be surprised at how much detail you will have about the "past" year. Make it up exactly as you want it to be. Do not compromise here.

Aligning Your Goals to Support Your Dream

Let's recap what you've accomplished thus far. Standing in your purpose, you have created a dream in at least one area of your life. You've made an honest assessment of where you are and where you want to be, and you've listened to your Doubter without allowing doubt and fear to limit your dream. You've stepped through the Sliding Glass Door and committed to your Dreamer. Now, as you're creating projects that will move you into action and demonstrate your belief in your desires, go back and have a look at the other areas of your life to ensure that they line up as well.

As you create a project, if it seems inconsistent or incompatible with other areas of your life—perhaps you're worried that you're selling out in one situation in order to have another—check to see whether your concern is real, or whether it's a negative attitude or belief. For example, if the hours you've designated for your project add up to more than twenty-four each day, you have an inconsistency that might require you to go back to the drawing board. If they add up to six or eight hours a day, and you're also working a full-time job, and one of your other dreams is to have more time for your family, there might be a problem there as well—perhaps not an insoluble one, but one that will require a creative strategy. If, on the other hand, the hours are available to you, but you're still troubled about having enough time for everything, acknowledge that the issue comes from an old belief. That's when you need to make a commitment that you will use your time in support of having your dream.

One of my clients, Ilene, had once been a professional dancer, studying under Alvin Ailey. Now, her dream was to quit her job and run her own dance company. When we got to the projects phase, Ilene kept bumping up against what seemed like a major conflict. How could she finance her new venture and support herself at the same time? She feared severing her ties with the people at her current place of employment. This required some creative thinking, but it was not an insurmountable obstacle. In fact, together we were able to design a strategy that enabled her to resign her full-time position, still pay her bills, and retain her relationship with her employer. I'd call that a win-win-win. The way we did it was to identify a skill that she was passionate about—grant proposal writing—that she could use as a freelancer. Once she realized she didn't need to be a salaried employee, she turned her current employer into her client, and generated twenty-five thousand dollars of income for herself within the first few weeks after she was on her own.

By admitting her fears to herself, and to me, Ilene was able to create a strategic solution. Once she knew how she would pay the rent, she turned her attention to the projects that would support her new venture. These included assembling a board, auditioning dancers, and scheduling recitals. The first major performance of Ilene's dance company, which I'm pleased to say I attended, was offered to an audience of more than two hundred people.

Don't be afraid to look at your life holistically; all of its components, including the dreams, are—or need to be—working together. Get a picture of it as a whole; perhaps there's a piece that's missing from your picture, like Ilene's grant-writing skill, that would tie things together to give you more time, money, and/or flexibility.

Streamline Your Strategy

Now that you know what your project is, all you have to do is figure out how you're going to make it happen! There are multiple ways of completing any project or achieving any end result. To make your project part of your reality, you will need strategies and steps to guide you toward your dream.

Some of us are great dreamers, but a little lacking in the strategy department. And some of us are brilliant strategists, but need a little practice dreaming. I think we should pump up both muscles, both sides of our brain. Let's dream and imagine *and* be practical and strategic. Let's dream and make our dreams come true.

A strategy is the approach or plan you will use to actually achieve your dream. Tactics are the specific step-by-step items to accomplish the strategy. Sometimes, when an entire project is put on a "to do" list, the project is actually composed of four or five separate tactics; if the separate tasks aren't listed individually, the project might never happen. As a matter of fact, the number one way a big or long-term dream dies is when we put it on a "to do" list as one unmanageable item. It must be broken down into small, manageable steps; steps we can actually accomplish and schedule, or we'll probably never attain the dream.

Once you get clear about the project, you can explore the strategies and steps you will need to accomplish it. For example, I decided to create one called, "Book At Least One Free and Fun Cruise to an Exotic Place within the Next Month." Then I listed the ways I could make it happen. In this case, I couldn't have taken what would be a normal first step, to purchase a ticket for the cruise, because my project was to go on a *free* cruise. It's important to be clear about what you want. One set of strategies might be needed to go on a fun cruise, while a different set is required to go on a *free* and fun cruise.

I chose to create a bartering relationship by booking a speech on a cruise ship in return for a free trip. Other strategies I could have chosen might include finding someone who would pay for my trip or entering a contest to win a free cruise.

Once I'd identified a strategy, the steps to accomplish it were clear: list and describe some topics about which I could speak; prepare my biography; get the name and number of several cruise ship lines which might be interested in such an arrangement; and so on. I decided to focus my energy on a certain cruise ship, rather than mass-mailing my proposal. I wanted the best cruise I could find, so I committed to getting booked by Cunard Lines, which owns the luxury liner, Queen Elizabeth II.

Because I was passionate about what I was doing, I was feeling equally powerful about accomplishing the results. I was definitely in action. In a period of three weeks, I developed promotional materials, sent out a package, and scheduled a date by which I wanted to set sail. Before I had a chance to make a follow-up call to see if they were interested, they called me. I was booked to go on the cruise five months ahead of what I had scheduled.

If I can make this kind of thing happen, so can you. Follow these simple "Designing a Blueprint" directions and walk through the process.

Designing a Blueprint

Here is a formula for putting any project into action:

1. Overview what's needed. Get the big, yet clear picture.
2. Break the project down into simple, manageable steps and strategies.
3. Identify your resources. Be creative.
4. Add dates and resources to each step.
5. Put in chronological order.
6. Assess where you might be overscheduled and where you can reorganize.
7. Be in action on your dream every day.

Don't Take the Long Route

I'm a great advocate of simplification and shortcuts. If you can find a faster way of getting something done, do it. One of your strategies might be to accomplish something you don't know how to do, and one of your tactics might be to learn it. However, another approach might be to hire or partner with somebody who already has that knowledge. Don't take the long route when you can see a shortcut.

A few years ago, I worked with a woman named Monica, who had been successful on Wall Street, making a six-figure salary. Now she was starting a whole new life: she was simultaneously pregnant with her first child, and leaving the world of stocks and bonds to start a new business. She was absolutely committed to her dream of having quality personal time with her friends and family, while developing and building a new business—she was determined to have a balanced life.

A successful person is often also an overcommitted person, and Monica fit the description. She was aware she had designed so much into her life that there wasn't room to create anything new. Therefore, we began by cleaning out the clutter, working with the "no more, now what?" as well as some completion exercises from the last chapter. We moved things out of the way, consolidated, organized, and created space, not just physically but emotionally, mentally, and spiritually.

Finally, Monica had *room* to design a whole new future, and we were ready to create projects and strategies.

Monica's range of projects included attending weekly prenatal classes, developing a marketing strategy for her new business, decorating a nursery, building a website, and spending quality time with her husband. Even with all the clutter-clearing we'd done, it was a daunting list. That's when we decided to get strategic.

Our best strategy was to double-up wherever possible to allow Monica more time. For example, one tactic that permitted her simultaneously to enjoy her pregnancy and to have quality time with her husband was to take a daily walk with him. Later, we turned this technique into a project with the goal of walking two hundred miles before the baby was born. This project supported Monica's needs for a healthy body and baby, for exercise and relaxation, and for time with her spouse.

Monica's issue wasn't only about balancing time; it also was about balancing energy so she would have enough to give to both areas of her life. Her commitment was to be the best she could be personally and professionally, without selling out on herself. Once we cleared the clutter, clarified her dreams, and created a strategy, the steps she needed to take became obvious.

Monica decided she was only going to work a certain number of days during the week. She built a lot of flexibility into that decision by allowing herself to choose weekly which days that would be. She also knew she would need some help to achieve the flexibility she wanted; she decided to hire a live-in housekeeper/nanny. That relieved her of both the concern about childcare while she was at the office, and the need to perform household chores. Thus, when she came home from her new business, she had the time and energy to be with her family. Her commitment to her dreams enabled her to create a balanced life using the resources at hand, a life she chose deliberately and loved living. Her story is a great illustration of how thinking strategically can resolve apparent conflicts in surprising ways.

Perhaps you're thinking, that's all very well for Monica, but I can't afford the luxury of hiring a housekeeper. You'd be surprised at how much can be accomplished through barter arrangements, like my cruise. Perhaps there is a student seeking housing who would live in your spare room in return for doing household chores or childcare. Commitment comes in many different forms. Get creative and dreamstorm. It's up to you.

When I go away on vacation, I often do it in a barter situation: for example, I traded speaking to the guests at the Red Mountain Spa for a retreat for two. With one phone call, I moved ahead on several of my dreams in one fell swoop, including: to live a spa life, have more fun and adventure, inspire people to dream, be healthy and fit, and create surprises in my relationship. That's the kind of thing that happens when you turn your life right-side-up! Aligned with your purpose, you will find there is often overlap on your projects. This means as you check off one activity, you might progress on many dreams simultaneously. The bartering opportunities never existed before I became clear about what I wanted and what I was committed to; now they exist regularly, and tie together many of the aspects of my life.

The more shortcuts you find, the more you will free yourself up. The more of yourself you have, the more you can put into your projects, and, don't forget, your projects are a way for you to project your dreams into the world. Schedule time for your dreams and for the things that make you happy.

Your Greatest Resource

One of your most powerful inner resources for moving forward on your projects is your own creativity, your ability to imagine and interpret. Be willing to try on something new. Make requests of other people that are beyond what you thought were initially impossible. Get up an hour earlier or an hour later. Flip through magazines you don't normally read. Find new ways to see things by trying on someone else's glasses, or closing your eyes and finding a new perspective. There are many methods of breaking out of your familiar worldview; you only need to look for them, experiment, and try them. For example, there are a variety of ways to look at your current life and the resources that you already have available. Make a list of "Resources I Haven't Yet Considered." Perhaps there are resources among the people who supply you with goods or services. Maybe there's something you can tap into at your alma mater, through special courses and seminars you've attended, or teachers you've had. Think about all the places you go during your week. Think about all the cities in all the countries where you know people, or have met people in the past.

Everything in your life is a resource, most especially yourself—the books you read, the movies you watch, the ideas you have, the energy you give off, the dreams you have when you sleep at night. Everything you experience is a resource you can use. How are you engaged with life? How are you using your resources? Remember, your creativity is your own greatest resource.

One often overlooked resource is perhaps the most obvious one. When we act as a resource for others, a kind of symbiosis can occur. It might not always happen immediately or even in the way you imagine it, but being generous and supportive of others can sometimes be the best and most abundant resource of all.

CHAPTER 12
Master Your #1 Shortcut

*A burning purpose attracts others who are drawn along
with it and help fulfill it.*

—Margaret Bourke-White

Some people still harbor old beliefs that they have to do everything themselves. If you feel that standing on your own two feet means never accepting help from anyone, it's important to acknowledge that tendency. Of course, you *can* "go it alone" if you insist, but it's a longer, harder process. Remember, you want to simplify the journey to having your dream, not complicate it. If you're part of a winning team, you can accelerate progress and expand your horizons—in short, it's easier and faster to do it with other people. In fact, I have found the number one way to experience greater ease in achieving any dream is to build a team. Remember how we talked about shortcuts? Well, this is the ultimate shortcut.

When I speak of a team, I don't necessarily mean a club or a group of people that meets with regularity, or even your work team. A formal group has potential for some people and not for others. Rather, I think of a team as a resource group, people to whom you can turn when you need advice, when you need a sounding board, when you need to unravel a thorny problem, or when you just need someone to listen. It might include many people you already know or work with, or people you've yet to meet. Although we tend not to want to bother others or recruit assistance, what happens whenever two or more are gathered is uncanny. I personally believe you're only a few phone calls away from anyone in the world you need to contact, and of course, now with social media you can access anyone. Use this to your advantage.

Letting others help you is not selfish—in fact, it's a form of true generosity, because you enable them to feel good about contributing to your success. Many people love to make a difference by helping others. You can allow people to assist you most effectively by learning how to make powerful requests. Get clear about what you need, find the individuals who can help you get it, and ask for what you want.

The Most Profound Tool: Enrollment

Of all the skills I've learned in my three decades of teaching how to achieve your dreams, this one is the most important. In order to master manifestation, you must master the skill of enrollment. By "enrollment," I'm referring to your ability to share your dreams, products, services, and ideas in a way that will inspire others to join you, hire you, and perhaps even invest in you. The obstacle called, "I don't have enough money" often disappears when you become good at enrollment. If the best shortcut step for accomplishing your dreams is to build a team, the key skill to develop is enrollment.

In all your interactions, be highly intentional, explore all possibilities and make every conversation count. I'm not saying you should see everyone as a tool to use for your own benefit. I'm saying you should see everyone as a fellow traveler on the road making their dreams come true. Like you, they are always looking for inspiration, encouragement, an uplifting view, a new idea, a refreshing way to view the world around them. By sharing your gifts, dreams, and opportunities, you will open up amazing conversations with others— and who knows where they could lead for both of you. One of my daily practices is to enroll people in believing in themselves. I do this by seeing their beauty and greatness, then acknowledging it.

What do I get in return? I feel loved as I practice being loving and generous. How simple it is to lift another up simply by recognizing their greatness. And since we are connected, the more I admire and appreciate them, the more I feel appreciated and loved.

Enrollment requires that you learn to speak like a visionary. A visionary has a big dream, articulates it with clarity so people get it, expresses it with passion so others get excited about it, and enrolls/invites others to join him or her. To be a successful enroller, you need to find your genuine voice and express the truth of who you are, what you believe, and what's in your heart. Enrollment happens when you express what matters to you and why you care—and you show others why they should, too.

As a big dreamer, your ability to enroll people in taking action is essential. This is not selling, convincing, or even trying. It is inspiring others by showing them the value of what you are doing, creating, or offering, and making a persuasive case for why they should help or join you.

One of the ways to be persuasive and compelling is to stand out as uniquely you. I was invited to speak at a conference recently where I was one of fourteen speakers. As the "new person" in the lineup, I was the last to take the stage. Wearing a dress and leopard print pumps, I half-jokingly announced that I was the chick without PowerPoint. I got a standing ovation just for that, for being different. And if you're wondering how that translates into real dollars and real business, I closed fifty percent of the room on my offer. The most any of the "guys" closed was twenty-five percent. Being uniquely you and valuing your story sets you apart from all the others. Do you want to be another one or *the* one?

I have two enrollment approaches to teach you. Both are effective and although they sound similar there is a different quality to each.

The Traditional Enrollment Approach

For decades I've taught this logical, left-brain, four-step approach. It's tried and true and the only way to get good at it is to practice.

Step 1: Establish rapport. This is the likeability factor. If people don't like and trust you it's unlikely they will proceed any further. Be authentically yourself. Show up as a person of integrity. The more you know who you are, what your values are, and what your purpose is, the more you will attract kindred spirits and like-minded individuals.

Step 2: Build value. People buy, say yes to, or invest in that which is valuable to them. In order to know what's valuable to an individual or group, you need to know what's important to them. You can ask or do your homework ahead of time. Often I hear people list off the features of what they have to offer. For example, someone selling an online course might explain how many days or hours it is, how many pages are in the workbook, or how many video modules are included. Although it is important that any offer is clear, we don't buy features, we buy benefits. And a confused mind doesn't buy at all. A simple practice to move from features toward benefits is this: after you say anything, add the phrase, "And what's so great about that is . . ." Say it out loud or silently think it and what you say next will most likely be value-based.

Step 3: Overcome objections. The two most common objections are time and money. The obstacle called money, or "this is too expensive," can be eliminated when you are providing more value than you're charging. Make it clear you have something they want or need, something valuable. (This is inevitably linked to your own self-worth and how you value your gifts and your time.) The best way to overcome objections is to do more of steps one and two—establish more rapport and build more value.

Step 4: Come to an agreement. You know the conversation is complete when you both or all agree on a clear next step. Are you scheduling a date for your next meeting? Will you be calling the other person or sending a contract? Is the other person signing on the dotted line, making a call, or writing a check? Even if you agree not to move forward, wrap the conversation up with gratitude and integrity.

The Heart-Centered Enrollment Approach

I've taught this traditional enrollment approach for many, many years to thousands of people all over the world. It's effective and it works. However, last year at my big annual event, the Wealthy Visionary Conference, I created and taught another method. It was a game-changer.

I came out on the stage to an audience of close to one thousand people. The theme was "Bridging Money & Meaning." Some people were attending because they had wealth and were seeking a greater expression for it, but most were there because they had important dreams and needed more money and resources for implementation. I saw immediately that the sooner I taught them enrollment, the sooner they would be meeting each other, identifying what they needed, and having heartfelt conversations about how they could help each other.

I found myself teaching a more feminine, heart-centered approach to enrollment. And there was no question that it was effective for both men and women. We generated over two million dollars in sales in the room as people found partners, sponsors, investors, clients, and more. Here's the process I taught.

Step 1: Connect to what you care about. If you don't care, why should anyone else? This is the context for the conversation. You are telling and/or showing me why you care and why I should as well. If I don't care, you either haven't communicated it clearly or I'm not a candidate for this conversation.

Step 2: Communicate your vision and ideas clearly. If someone doesn't easily get what you're trying to communicate, rather than tell you they don't get it, most people will just check out. Practice being clear and succinct while also expressing your passion and care. Set an intention for the conversation or the phone call before you initiate it.

Step 3: Make a compelling invitation for others to join you *now*. There is something to be said for urgency. Give people a reason to act now. In business, it's usually an expiration date, or a discount or bonus for acting today. But even outside of business, if you can ask people for a commitment as to when they'll do something or get back to you, you're more likely to see a positive outcome or result and you'll know when it's done. Conversations and relationships left hanging or open-ended can be a source of misunderstanding and even suffering. As we discussed in chapter ten, leaving something incomplete can prevent you from moving forward. Wrap up the loose ends.

Whichever approach you choose, have confidence that you will succeed. There are many reasons why others would be interested in participating with you. After all, you're a go-getter with a big dream; in its completion, your dream will benefit others. What happens out of enrollment is beyond anything you can imagine. Invite people to be on your team. If they don't know you are looking for support, they can't give it. It's up to you to make the first move and ask. And here's a tip: *Make it really easy for them to say yes.*

My client Judy was a talented singer and performer, but had decided early in her career to postpone her music dreams and marry a wonderful man. Although she sang in her church choir, her main focus in life was to be a great wife and mom. Her family and home were her first priority. She was grateful she could provide marketing services for the singer Tony Orlando in the town of Branson, Missouri, where she lived. But as she went through the dream process outlined in this book, it became very clear that she was a singer at heart. This was a well-kept secret, however, especially from Tony.

Once Judy decided to pursue her dream, she took several important steps to make it happen. But perhaps the most important step was enrolling the biggest resource she knew: Tony. Most nights, when Tony performed, he would walk out into the audience and hand the microphone to various people inviting them to sing a bit. One night, Judy, who showed up often to Tony's shows, motioned for him to give her the mic. He was surprised and a little confused, but only for a moment; he was shocked at the beautiful voice that was coming out of Judy. She was then able to tell him that she had a dream and wanted his help; the next time they met up, she made a very specific request. "I want to be in your show. Can I?" Opening night of his Christmas show, "Santa & Me," it happened. Tony said to Judy, "You, every show, starting tomorrow."

A Life-Saving Skill

When Victoria Ferro came to America from the Philippines, she had nothing but a dream and an outsized dose of determination. And her dream was a serious one: to get the best possible treatment in order to beat the cancer that was growing in her breast.

I met Victoria at my Conference. After hearing me speak some weeks earlier, she had found a way to be there even though she didn't have a job or an income. She later told me that my techniques for enrollment were the most powerful skills she'd ever learned. When she got home, Victoria took everything she'd learned and sat down to write the most important letter of her life.

For some time, she had been trying, unsuccessfully, to get treatment at Stanford Medical Center. But with no money and no insurance, she had been turned away repeatedly. Now, she was ready to take another shot. In the letter, she described her case in great detail, and explained why it was her dream to be treated at Stanford. She even included a photograph of her large and visible tumor. That same day, she got a call from the medical center: the doctor wanted to see her that very afternoon.

In her passionate letter, Victoria successfully enrolled the doctor who is now giving her life-saving treatment. She used those same skills to get health insurance, despite her non-resident status, to receive several grants, and even to find a place to live. And she's now contributing her powers of persuasion to an amazing cause, working for a nonprofit that helps other low-income cancer sufferers. (You can read more about the story of this organization, founded by my client Mike Murphy, in chapter fifteen.) Her health continues to improve, and her faith and positive attitude are inspirational. For Victoria, learning how to enroll others was not just a shortcut to her dream—it was, as she puts it, "the thing that saved my life."

Just Ask

The key to enrollment is your ability to make requests. Ask for something specific; the more precise the request, the more specific the response. And make it easy for people to say yes. People typically say no when you ask for too much or they don't understand the request.

Simply say, "I'd like to make a request of you." I have found the most powerful way is to say something like, "Would you be willing to explore . . ." Your query can be accepted or declined, or the other person can make a counter-offer.

I used this line to great effect one day recently, and in so doing, managed to fulfill one of my lingering dreams. While speaking at the Golden Door Spa, I had decided to squeeze in a workout, so I headed over to the gym and on to the treadmill. With my short legs, a twelve-minute mile (on a good day) is more like walking, but nonetheless, I celebrate my effort.

I was soon joined by a tall, attractive woman whose legs seemed as long as my entire body. She proceeded to do something I've never seen anyone do on a treadmill. She sprinted. I did the only self-respecting thing I knew to do. I turned off my machine and cheered her on.

"You go, girl," I shouted. When she was done, I tossed her a towel and we laughed. "Who are you and where did you learn to run like that?" I asked.

"My name is Marty Evans," she replied. "I'm a retired Rear Admiral for the Navy."

"What do you do now?" I queried.

"I'm the National Director for the Girl Scouts of America."

When the door of opportunity opens, be prepared, even with the dreams that are on your "maybe someday" list.

Mine was, "Someday, I'll start an inner city Dream Camp where kids will not only experience ropes courses and cookouts, but learn the important skills for realizing their dreams."

Now I was being offered a shortcut. I just had to ask the question.

"Marty, I teach people how to achieve their dreams and one of mine is to help kids. Would you be willing to explore having me do some work with the Girl Scouts?"

"Sure," she replied with a warm smile.

Now I can be found several times throughout the year sleeping in a tent. Teaching teenage girls is rich and profound, and I have the privilege of doing it simply because I asked.

When you make a request, be willing to hear what people say in response. When you ask for something, you signal to others that your interest in what they have to offer is more than casual and they are likely to take you more seriously. You convey the message you'd like to have an answer, that you're interested in moving the conversation and, possibly, the relationship forward. Once you've got someone's attention, you can enlist his or her services in several ways. As I've mentioned before, one of my favorite methods is to barter or trade services. One woman I know conducts public relations activities for her Certified Public Accountant in exchange for accounting assistance. Someone else trades strategic planning services for massage therapy, or coaching for cooking. If you think you don't have anything to barter, reexamine what you're passionate about. Most of us can offer some kind of service in exchange for another. It's a great way of experiencing what you're capable of doing and to value your gifts.

A Global Team Effort

I've been on both sides of the enrollment conversation. One person who successfully enrolled me in her dream was Gillian Rudd, head of the U.S. contingent of the World Association of Women Entrepreneurs. Her dream was to invite women business owners from all over the world to Washington, D.C., where they would be treated to a special event.

Gillian described her dream to me and I became excited about it and agreed to be part of her team. Together, we organized a group of women to dreamstorm around her idea. I helped her clarify the dream and turn it into a more concrete event. We decided to hold a major luncheon and international media event in the nation's capital at the National Press Club. The objective of this event was to honor women entrepreneurs from thirty countries throughout the world, and to have them recognized by other women business owners, corporations, government officials, and the media. The exposure and visibility was expected to garner greater national attention for the organization, additional funds, an increase in U.S. membership, and a boost to the organization's international membership.

As the brainstorming continued, we decided to create the Declaration of International Partnership. We developed a document that focused on five areas in which women business owners could make an impact: education, environment, enterprise, communication, and innovation. Some five hundred people attended the sellout event and you could hear a pin drop as each of the thirty country presidents signed the document. It was hailed as a historic event, and got major television and print exposure, including the international edition of *USA Today*. And just for the record, there was no budget available for producing this stellar event. Funds were raised and corporate sponsors signed on because it was an amazing vision expressed with great passion. Every dream starts with an idea and grows proportionately to the amount of energy, excitement, and commitment behind it. Enrollment is key for greater impact and real results.

Share Your Dream with Anyone, Anytime, Anywhere

I know there are schools of thought that say you should not indiscriminately share your dreams and I respect that. But if you are not sharing your dreams with that many people, you might be missing some wonderful and unexpected opportunities for help. This is why I believe you should share your dream with anyone, anytime, anywhere. You never know how they might respond and who might resonate with your dream and become part of your team.

Of course, there are those negative people in your life, the dream-stealers or dream-killers, who you need to be aware of. But even they can become part of your team. One woman told me that her own mother is so negative that she stopped sharing her dreams with her. Then one day she had this insight. "If everything in life serves a function, I wonder what my mother's negative attitude could serve?" She got it. Whenever she is ready to launch a new product or service, she calls her mother. As expected, her mom tells her everything that could possibly go wrong. This woman then designs strategies to manage all those potential obstacles. She overcame her limiting belief about her mother's negativity and found a way to use and benefit from it. She now considers her mother a key member of her team.

Speaking of mothers, it's important to talk to all of your family members about your dream. Sometimes we feel absolutely sure that we cannot get the support we want from the people whom we want it most. Don't let that belief stop you. Let them change their minds. Any day, any moment could be the moment they sign up to be on your team. Let them hear your commitment and enthusiasm, and be unstoppable regardless of how they respond. Demonstrate your commitment by taking action. There really is no other way. As other people see your commitment, no matter how big the dream might be, eventually they will stand behind you. Tenacity often yields credibility. Show them you're not giving up; ask them to support you, even if it's only by believing in you, and be open to receiving their support.

When you think about involving your family, notice your attitudes and beliefs. Is that voice inside your head saying, "My parents never thought I could do it" or "my sensible sister will think I'm off on another hair-brained scheme"? Those are just your attitudes and beliefs; you can go back and transform them using the techniques we learned in chapter eight but you don't have to include them in what you are designing for the future.

Be clear about what you're committed to and start to speak it powerfully so that people around you can help. Get others on board, whether they play an intimate role in your dream or a tangential one. It's all part of building a winning team.

Speak about your dreams at work. You never know what support or resources you might find in your own company or workplace. Here are some questions you might consider: With whom can you speak about your dream when you go to work tomorrow? Is your boss enrolled? Your co-workers? Do they even know that you have a dream? Have you already decided that they're not potential partners and they can't help you? Or are you sitting there thinking that you can't pursue your dream without your boss's support, even though your boss might not know what your dream is? Don't kill off possibilities before you've explored them. Look for ways to share your dream and tie it into the other aspects of your life.

Lynn had been working in her position as a vice president of marketing for many years. She was burned out and knew exactly what she wanted. Her dream was to have fifty-two vacation days a year without cutting her salary. Her task, therefore, was to enroll the president of the company. She made her proposal to the president, who at first had a hard time swallowing it. But Lynn was skilled at painting a clear picture and was able to outline the benefits. She pointed out how she could get the company operating at maximum efficiency and relayed that she would train her staff to function well, without her being there on a day-to-day basis.

When Lynn took a little more time, she got crystal clear about her true dream. What she really wanted, what she was really passionate about, was travel. This meant she needed freedom and flexibility. Getting an extra day off here and there or going to a four-day workweek was not what she needed. Once again, Lynn shared her dream with her boss and started to prepare the people under her for the transition. When the negotiations were done, she got what she wanted. She went part-time, working 80 percent of her original schedule, without any cut in pay.

Then she realized there was something that she had left on the table. Her company barters with United Airlines by trading baked goods for airline tickets. If she could get some of those tickets that would be a dream come true. She went back in and told her boss there was one more thing that would really make her happy. They agreed she could have eight of the free round-trip tickets to help fulfill her dream of world travel. The lesson? Ask for what you want.

When you share your dream, it's okay also to speak about your fears and concerns. If others are facing the same fears and concerns, the issues can be put on the table for discussion. You might recall that, in chapter six, we spoke of the importance of honesty about your current reality; sharing that truth with another person can be an insightful experience. Just be sure to keep your fears and concerns under the heading "where I am now" and not let them seep into your dream.

Trust, let the conversation flow, and listen to what is being said. Something new might show up: perhaps they know of a new resource; maybe they will suggest a new way for you to look at something. Don't be rigidly attached to what is already in your mind. In speaking your dream, new opportunities will show up. Keep your eyes and ears open. Expect success.

It Takes a Team

It's rare that I come across a dream or project that wouldn't benefit from a team. I'm also often asked by skeptics, "Can you really design a strategy and create a team for achieving any dream, even finding a new relationship?" The answer is, yes—I've seen it happen. One of my favorite examples is Gwen. By the time she hit her mid-thirties, Gwen's professional life was sailing along, but there was a new dream that was taking precedence. She wanted to be in a loving relationship with her dream man and have a family. She realized for this to happen she needed to share her dream and build a solid team who would help her.

Gwen decided to send an email to twenty of her friends and associates. She wrote:

I am sending you this note with three specific requests:

1. *Will you be on my Dream Team? (Yes means that you will hold my dream in your heart and check in with me to see that I am taking action on my dream.)*

2. *Please read my vision of the kind of relationship that I am seeking and the qualities of a man that I desire.*

3. *Please introduce me to any and all eligible bachelors that you believe are potential candidates for a match with me. I trust you.*

Her email went on to include her wish list and closed by saying this: "The more I voice who I am, what I am seeking, and what I love, the sooner I will have what my heart desires." Her friends responded very supportively (always the sign of true friends). They told her they thought this was a bold move and would help her. Gwen has been having lots of dates and continues to share her dream. I recently called her for an update and she said there is now a new man in her life.

So, yes, you can create a team to help achieve any dream you might have—and trust me, it will get you there faster than you could ever have gotten there alone.

Who's Enrolling You in Believing in Yourself?

There are profound resources out there that can help you clarify and create what you want. I am one of them, and there are many others as well. As you think about creating your team, consider whether working with a high-level coach might be an investment you want to make. A seasoned and intuitive coach can not only help you gain greater clarity about what you want, he or she can also truly see you, feel you, and guide you. A huge part of my work as a coach is about seeing people in ways they cannot see themselves, and then enrolling them in believing in themselves.

The way I work one-on-one with clients is in what I call Visionary Strategy Days. These high-level sessions involve my five-step protocol, where I take clients deep into their souls to uncover their purpose and align their lives with it. From there, I help them define and articulate a new or expanded vision. We uncover any blocks, obstacles, issues, limiting beliefs, or concerns and remove them. And we design projects, practices, and brilliant shortcuts they can use, including mapping out a 30-90 day action plan. Finally, I leave no stone unturned, taking them through role-playing exercises in which they communicate their vision, to ensure they leave with clarity and confidence.

I've had the privilege over the last thirty years to work with many extraordinary people from every walk of life. And what I can tell you for certain is this: almost every time when they walk in and I ask what their intention is for the day, the first word out of their mouths is clarity. "I want greater clarity about my destiny, my mission, and my calling, but also a strategy and plan for how I can monetize my dreams and my ideas." Sometimes, it's hard to get this kind of clarity by yourself. Sometimes we are so close to who we are and what we do, that we don't see what is unique, special, and valuable about it, much less how to get there.

Let me give you a few stories and examples of people who have worked with me and what they've accomplished. These three examples happen to be a trio of powerful women, although I have coached many men as well, including executives and entrepreneurs.

Anastasia Chopelas was a powerful healer, but she was reluctant to talk about herself in that context. The main reason for this was that for decades she's been a world-class high-end scientific researcher. She has degrees from Caltech and UCLA and conducted research at UCLA, the University of Washington, UNLV, and the Max Planck Institute for Chemistry in Mainz, Germany. She had data, statistics, and all kinds of information to back up what she knew and was practicing, but she was worried people wouldn't take her seriously. In listening to her and tuning in to her heart, what I saw was that she should be branded as "The Scientific Healer." Once we did that, all of her questions were answered, including how to speak about the work she did, have enrollment conversations, even create pricing structures. It was my ability to see the gold in who she was and even in her hesitation that allowed me to create the brand that set her apart from everyone else. She said she now has "clear guidance in writing my book and developing programs in a coherent way that are aligned with my purpose."

Another woman I worked with, a coach named Deborah Olive, was struggling with, as she put it, "how to funnel thirty years of experience into language that revealed the value of what I deliver to future clients." My process made it easy for her to see what made her completely unique, remove key obstacles, identify the common thread in the results she delivered, and clarify her ideal client. It was funny – when I branded her "The Big Coach," she got a little self-conscious initially. Of course, the URL was waiting for her, but she asked, "How do I even talk about this?" Often, the second half of my Visionary Strategy Days are about role-playing so the client feels comfortable expressing the new label or brand I've given them.

Deborah basically learned how to say, "If you have a big vision and want big results, you need me because I'm The Big Coach." She immediately secured three new clients at a higher rate than she had ever charged before. She added that now she is clear and really owning her new brand, her words and energy are congruent. And it was only through someone else's eyes that she was able to see who she truly was. Once we branded her, all of her friends said, "Well, of course that's who you are."

One final story is about Joyce Rosenblad. Joyce had been somewhat successful as a stylist for many years, but it didn't feel like she was really living into the depth of her soul. With my insight and coaching, we rebranded her. I dubbed her "The Sacred Stylist" because it was really true about who she was. I could see it in her eyes and hear it in her voice. The more we role-played this, the more I drew that out of her. In a matter of hours she really came into alignment with her new sense of identity and purpose. She said this was "the best investment I've ever made in my business." Not only did she immediately make back the investment, she now is living into her essential self. In fact, she declared, "The investment will return to me ten-fold, not only monetarily, but in living a life filled with meaning and passion."

We could say all I did was add the word "sacred," but just as finding the perfect word for your purpose statement can completely change how you live your life, finding the perfect brand that is the expression of your heart, your essential self, and on purpose, is a game-changer for anyone professionally. Please keep in mind, I don't market myself as a branding expert, although I have branded many individuals and companies over the last years. Rather, I'm using an intuitive and creative process to truly see them, and help them be revealed to themselves; then through designing short-term strategies, putting together a menu of services, and most importantly, helping them find a simple, authentic, and powerful way to speak about it, their businesses and lives are being transformed, as are so many of the lives of the people that touching around them.

CHAPTER 13
Do What You Love

*All prosperity begins in the mind and is dependent only
upon the full use of our creative imagination.*

—Ruth Ross, *Prospering Woman*

There's never been a better time to pursue your dream, do what you love, and even get paid well for it. That's right. No matter what's going on in the economy, it *is* possible to not only get paid but get paid well for doing what you love.

I know there are a lot of naysayers who wouldn't agree with me. But they are probably the same people who are still trading time for dollars, feeling chained to their desks. They don't realize it doesn't have to be like that. In this chapter, I'll be sharing proven powerful tools to help you live a life where you have the freedom to do the things you love, and even turn your dreams into dollars, if that's what you want.

I am often asked if I believe every passion can be turned into a business. I believe it *can* be, but it doesn't have to be. For some, taking what you love and turning it into a vocation would kill the passion. For others, being paid for doing what you love would be the ultimate dream come true.

When I was a guest on *The Oprah Winfrey Show,* Oprah walked out into the audience and asked people to name their passion. My job was to suggest, on the spot, a business idea that would allow them to turn their passion into a profession. One woman said, "I love to cook and to travel." I inquired if she would consider being a traveling chef. She now cooks aboard a cruise ship.

A client of mine, Kathleen, was a realtor whose passion was Italy. She lived, breathed, and dreamed about moving to Italy. I asked her if she could do anything at all, what would that be. She replied, "Marcia, the truth is I have two great loves. I love to walk and wander, and I love to cook and eat." Next time you are in Tuscany, look her up. She now leads walking tours and picnics in one of the most beautiful places in the world. Often the unexpected becomes obvious and available when you connect to your passion.

What I also shared that day on *Oprah,* was my conviction that some dreams shouldn't be turned into businesses. You don't have to charge for what you do unless you need to and/or want to. Many exquisite dreams are launched each day dedicated to being of service, making a contribution, or volunteering. But it's a fact that in our society money is useful and often needed in order to accomplish big dreams.

Do what you love because you are called to do it. If you want to turn it into a business but perhaps think your idea is too crazy, far-fetched, or no one will pay for what you have, here's my thought on that: If I could create a multi-million dollar business helping people achieve their dreams, anything is possible!

Finding Time

Time is a funny thing. Sometimes we feel that it's closing in around us, but when there's something we're passionate about, we create a way to make it happen. I often say that passion is the ultimate time-management tool because, when you're passionate about what you're doing, you can get so much more done. But for many people, their dream is to have more ease, space, and balance in their lives, not just accomplish more. I wrote my book *Doing Less and Having More* primarily because I so often heard people say, "Not only do I not have time to make my dreams happen, I don't even have time to know what my dreams are." I wanted to teach those people how to create lives with more time and greater ease.

Doing less is not about doing nothing. It is about being centered and balanced. It is about choice and freedom. And it is about ease. What is it you would like to do less of? Would you like to fret less? Would you like to have less stress and anxiety? Perhaps you would like to work less or waste less energy.

It takes focus and commitment to design your life to work this way. It takes time, too, to learn a completely new way to live, think, and plan. As you prepare to redesign your life, keep it simple at first, so you won't feel overwhelmed. Perhaps through reading this book you've begun to live on purpose in one area of your life, moving toward one dream that matters to you, initiating one project that will ignite your passion. If you schedule it, and it matters to you, I promise that you'll make the time to do it.

Even if you are employed by a company where most of the projects you work on have been assigned, you can still find one area where you're in control, then slowly begin to work on other areas. Maybe there's a project you can bring into your company; or a project that already exists to which you're not now assigned, but which is in alignment with your interests. If you're not passionate at work, think about what quality you can bring to your job that will allow you to express more passion there. Maybe there's a piece of something you feel passionate about that you can integrate into a work project, such as your love for learning or for helping others or for being creative.

One man I know, who has a passion for fun and baseball, turned a tedious task into a friendly, yet competitive game. He divided his colleagues into two teams, donned a referee shirt, put a whistle in his mouth and yelled, "Play ball!" which they did. A huge warehouse inventory was accomplished in record time and they all went out for beer afterward to celebrate.

If you can't infuse your job with passion, perhaps you are turned on by an issue in your community. Follow your passion. Pursue what has heart and meaning for you.

Simplify

As we discussed in chapter ten, if you have so many things going in your life that you need to clear some out before you can get to higher ground, there's something you can do about that: simplify. As you move forward with your dreams, you might need to keep coming back to the question, how can I simplify?

Go back to your purpose, the simple, broad expression of who you are, and revisit your dreams. Cross-reference that massive list of projects, and all the other things you've got going on, and see how they align with your dreams. Perhaps amid all that clutter there's actually something missing, an area left out of your dreams, such as having a balanced life.

Now you have another choice to make. You can add another dream, or you can take a critical look at your projects to see if you're committed to all of them. Perhaps they're not all on your "A" list. If you're compulsive about not giving anything up, and you decide that you're committed to everything, maybe there's something you don't absolutely have to do this year. Or, you might decide that it's fine to eliminate the four or five projects you feel burdened by, the ones that aren't even listed under a dream you think is important. Or you could get some help.

There is always a way to create a life that supports who you are, and there are always places where things can be relaxed. You can ease up in your desire to have something, your commitment to it, your schedule, or the degree to which you need to have it. It all starts with that foundation called your life's purpose: Who are you really and just what are you committed to?

An important conversation that I have with everybody that I work with is, "How do you *really* want your life to be?" When you get clear about the values that are most important to you, that impacts the decisions that you make. For example, I remember feeling torn and conflicted because on a spiritual level and in service to my purpose, I wanted to help as many people in the world as I possibly could. But in trying to do that, I burned myself out. I tried to be all things to all people and I ended up being not much to anyone, especially myself.

So I decided that I would use my Dream University® website to give away an entire library of content—hundreds of articles, audios, and videos that would help people get clear about their dreams, believe in their dreams, and act on their dreams. That decision gave me a lot of peace, knowing that I was living in integrity with my purpose, while concurrently opening myself up to have time for the caliber of people that I most want to work with and create the quality of life that is important to me. For example, I prefer to impact people who are impacting the world. I prefer to fly first class when I travel and be paid really well for the value and service I provide. I could have sabotaged my dream by saying, "If I'm charging a lot of money, I won't be living on purpose because I'll be excluding people." Instead, I created a solution and said, "My vision is to live on purpose and that includes being paid well and also being available for nonprofit work." Because I got more discerning, I'm actually making more money, working less, serving more people, and living a life that allows me the flexibility and freedom to be generous, spacious, and available.

The Myth of Prerequisites

As you've probably realized by now, one of my favorite parts of being a Dream Coach® is helping people find shortcuts to their dreams. Sometimes people become paralyzed by the belief that, to move on, they need to gain certain skills or additional assets first. I call this "the myth of prerequisites." When people let go of this myth, they find there are often resources readily available to help them move quickly through the process of getting their dream. They might just need to approach it from a different angle or think more creatively. One method, of course, is skill-building; another is finding or hiring somebody who has the skills to do it for you. Getting the advice of a coach, which we discussed in chapter twelve, is another great way to find a short cut.

Angela told me she always wanted to be a doctor, but she never could amass the time or money to go to medical school. When she got in touch with what made her feel passionate, she saw she wanted to work in the medical field, but she didn't want to be a doctor. When she was relieved of the burdens of facing how she would go through medical school, she quickly arranged for the training she needed to become an emergency medical technician. Now she's living her dream and saving lives.

I met another woman, Marilee, at a business function/cocktail party. She was eager to share her dream of moving from being a first-grade teacher to being a world-renowned clothing designer and I got caught up in her obvious passion. But I soon became exhausted as she mapped out for me what sounded like the longest, hardest road imaginable.

"Do you really think it needs to be that hard?" I asked.

She was intrigued and asked, "How would you do it?"

"Do you have talent? Are you good?"

"I'm very good," she replied, confidently.

"Then bank on your talent. Prove that you are more committed to your dream then you are to your reality or your doubt by taking action." I didn't tell her what to do, but I trusted if she followed my advice, she would find a shortcut. And sure enough, she did.

A few weeks later a package arrived at my home from Marilee with magnificent sketches of outfits for me. One was a hot pink skirt and pants suit, one was a short, sexy purple dress, and one was a red evening gown, with a caption under it that said, "I picture you wearing this for dinner at the White House." Although I have yet to be invited, I was relieved to know that I would have something to wear. And I loved that she was dreaming for me. I called her and said, "Make the outfits," which she did.

Besides purchasing the outfits, which looked great, I told some friends, and then the word was out. Marilee told me the greatest gift I gave her was when I said, "These are fabulous. I believe in your dream." With that vote of confidence, she enrolled in the Fashion Institute of Design Merchandising, and in less than three years and with an investment of seventeen thousand dollars, she graduated with a 4.0 grade point average.

Since then, Marilee has been invited to design women's golf wear, band uniforms, and at the Los Angeles County Museum of Art, someone wanted to buy the jacket off her back and produce a line of them. She's getting ready to submit her designs to a major clothing label, and I have no doubt that if she presents them with as much passion as she presented those first designs to me, she'll be hired.

Everyone has internal dialogues like Marilee had. We create long lists of prerequisites for pursuing our dreams. "I'll do it when I have the money, when I get the education, when my family's ready to support me, after my children are grown." But it's not always true that A must precede B. Avoid the myth of prerequisites and prove to life and yourself that you are serious. As you develop greater confidence and capability to say yes to what you truly want, life will affirm and assist you in ways you can't even imagine. What prerequisites have you put in your own way that slow you down or keep you from having your dream? Are they real? Are they necessary? Is there another way to move forward?

The Value of You

Initially when people heard the name of my big annual event was the Wealthy Visionary Conference, many assumed it wasn't for them, declaring they were neither wealthy nor a visionary.

If you have a dream, want to expand it to reach more people, make an impact with it, *and* monetize it, you have the mindset and the "heart-set" of a wealthy visionary. Rather than saying, "That's not me," acknowledge you are on a path of becoming this. We are all becoming a better version of ourselves.

Here's my five-step approach for being paid well for doing what you love.

> **Step 1. Do what you love.** Don't wait for circumstances to change or fall prey to the myth of prerequisites. Do it now.

> **Step 2. Value your gifts.** I'll say more about this in a moment.

> **Step 3. Charge what you're worth.** When you value your gifts and keep your agreements with yourself, you'll find the confidence to do this.

> **Step 4. Have powerful enrollment conversations.** See chapter twelve for more about this shortcut to your dreams.

> **Step 5. Repeat often!**

At the conference, we spent a fair amount of time looking at our value and self-worth and at where and how we determine it. Looking in your bank account is not the measurement of who you are or what you should believe is possible, but it might be a significant indicator of how you value your gifts.

Most people I know under-charge because of limiting beliefs. Perhaps you still believe that you have to "suffer to sing the blues." Maybe your work is of a spiritual nature and you think it's not noble or holy to charge for it. If that's you, please go back and revisit the chapter on changing your beliefs.

In this world we need money to survive and many use their jobs (which they don't like or complain about) in order to finance what they really want to do. This is one approach, but it is one that will leave your energy and attention painfully bifurcated. If you could be paid well for doing what you love, what changes would you make? What would you do more or less of? What would you do *now*?

At my event, there were many entrepreneurs and business executives but also some stay-at-home parents. These men and women admitted that it was challenging to cultivate a healthy self-worth because they weren't being paid to parent. But cash is only one form of payment. Gratitude, appreciation, pride, knowing that you have or are making a difference in another person's life—perhaps your spouse, child, or other family member—this too is valuable and sometimes even priceless. Value your gifts, however you are being compensated for them.

How you value yourself and what you bring to the table is critical to having others believe in you and your dreams. You have to believe first. If you are passionate about it, I wholeheartedly encourage you to act on it—now! Ask yourself, could I charge for this? Am I charging enough for my unique gifts and contributions? Here's an important tip if you're struggling with Step 3: When your intention and your integrity are in alignment, as we discussed in chapter nine, it will give you the confidence to charge more for what you do.

When I was president of the National Association of Women Business Owners in Washington, DC, the position afforded me some wonderful opportunities. One of my favorites was that I would often have the pleasure of meeting with women from all over the world. One afternoon I met Tatiana for tea. She was visiting from Russia.

"I envy you," she began, "because you are a woman business owner."

I was confused. "Tatiana, you're a woman, and you have a business. I don't get it."

"I don't charge for my services." She explained she was an art dealer, but she didn't believe her artists could afford to pay her.

I had an idea. "Tatiana, I am exploring doing business with your country. Can I ask you some questions?" She was eager to comply.

After about ten minutes, I thanked her and told her I believe in paying for information. At first she refused, but then she saw I was only holding a one-dollar bill in my hand. She laughed and took it.

I said, "You have just been paid for a service you provided. You are now a woman business owner."

A year went by before I saw her again. She strode in to my office and announced that now she was indeed a woman business owner.

"I went home and started to charge for my services. The amazing thing was they were willing to pay me. I now represent some of the finest artists in my country."

One of those artists, she told me, was a goldsmith. She proudly showed me a beautiful gold charm in the shape of a box that she was wearing on a chain around her neck. I could see that there was something inside it, and when I looked closer, I saw that it was a dollar bill.

"You believed in me before I did," she said. "But once you helped me see what was possible, and value myself, I knew it was what I wanted."

Do you believe in your own value? I believe in it—just as I believed in Tatiana's. Prove you believe in the value of your gifts and contributions by charging what you are worth, and in so doing, turn your dreams into dollars. It *is* possible—if you believe it.

CHAPTER 14

Trust Yourself

We convince by our presence.

—Walt Whitman

On the path to accomplishing your dreams, you're going to meet up with an issue called trust. Trust, a factor that's at the core of everything, either allows your dream to manifest or keeps it from happening in your life. Trust is important at every stage in the process, but it's particularly important when you confront the inevitable challenges that will show up as you take bigger risks, dream bigger dreams, and live a more impactful life.

The most important kind of trust is self-trust, which we discussed in chapter nine. Self-trust matters because the path to your dreams will take you into the unknown, and the path to the unknown is uncertainty. As you get more comfortable with uncertainty, you will be more willing to take risks, to dream, and to be wrong, which opens you up to greater possibilities. And the way to get comfortable with uncertainty is to trust yourself.

Self-trust comes from connecting to your heart-wisdom, not just your intellect. Self-trust comes from knowing who you are and being true to your purpose. Self-trust comes from integrity, opening your heart, facing your shadow, and speaking your truth.

I faced a major test in my own self-trust many years ago, when I bought what I thought was my dream home in the Bay Area. The views of the water and bridges were beautiful and although the half-renovated house needed work, I moved in. After a few months, it was time to install my dream bathroom and with the opening of a wall, the nightmare began. A wide, deep crack in a load-bearing wall sent my then-boyfriend and I searching for the cause. It turned out the previous owners failed to disclose they had built a false floor to conceal that the house had slipped eight inches on the foundation. The news got worse from there. The entire house had to come down.

Droves of lawyers were hired as a suit unfolded involving five parties; me, the sellers, both real estate agents, and the inspector, who had said, "You're buying a solid little house on a solid little slab." He was wrong.

As the tally for legal fees grew to thousands upon thousands of dollars, the sellers ran out of money and I wasn't far behind them. The question is: how long do you hang in there when the rules of the "blame game" are that (guilty or innocent) the last person standing wins?

We were frustrated, angry, and tormented as we continued to live in the rapidly deteriorating house, which we began to refer to as "the dump."

I continued to tour around the world speaking, but in my heart I felt like a fraud because while I was encouraging others to go for their dreams, I was feeling helpless and hopeless. I can be tenacious but sometimes strength becomes weakness. After four years of feeling like a victim, I finally put my foot down and said, "No more!" I demanded that my lawyer get me in front of a judge to hear my case.

When we met with the judge, he sympathetically looked me in the eye and said, "The law doesn't always protect the innocent. I recommend you get out from under this and get on with your life. If you go to court you could lose."

Shocked, we pulled the plug on the case and fired the lawyer, opting to walk away.

When we were originally told our old home had to be torn down, we dreamed of building a waterfront Mediterranean villa on the lot. As the house fell into further disarray and mold and mildew moved in, it was clearly past the time for us to move out. Tired of the ordeal, we opted to sell the property and buy a new house. I committed to finding a stunning Mediterranean villa that looked like the one we designed and would have built once the suit settled.

Sure enough, the first day I became intentional about moving, I found it. There it stood, right before my eyes. It was way out of our price range, but I could easily imagine living here as I pictured friends and community gathering, abundance and joy, and great success in our careers. This was the home in which to live the life of my dreams, and I named it the Dream Palace.

But my family and boyfriend loudly voiced their concerns that we couldn't buy until we sold the old house. I battled my own fears, thinking the new house was too expensive and this was not the right time. "Sell the old before you buy the new one," my Doubter chanted obsessively. I knew making this leap would forever change our lives, but with everyone warning me against it, I was afraid and confused, so I called my financial advisor seeking guidance and encouragement. He said, "I have good news and bad news. You worked your tail off these last four years (mostly to pay legal bills) so you do have enough for the down payment. The bad news is, you can't afford to carry two mortgages."

I hung up with such a heavy heart and tears in my eyes. I was clearly being tested—and it was a big one. I teach other people to pursue their dreams even when there is no evidence your dream is a good idea or that this is the right time to pursue it. I tell people not to look in their checkbooks or bank accounts to decide if they believe in their dreams. I challenge people to believe in something because it matters to them and then prove it really does by taking action. So this was the moment of truth for me. Would I be a hypocrite or an example? Would I trust myself and my dream, or would I listen to the doubts of everyone around me, and the voice of my Doubter?

"If we don't go for this dream," I explained to my partner, "then everything that I teach and speak about is a lie and my career is over."

Before he had a chance to respond, I grabbed him by the sleeve—and jumped. We bought our dream home. Yes, we were heading to paradise and happy, but also scared and saddled with two mortgages. Within a month we moved and while waiting for our furniture to arrive, spent our first romantic evening camped out on an air mattress in front of the fireplace with a bottle of champagne. As the morning light came flooding into the room, I let out a scream, waking him abruptly from a sound sleep.

"I know who is going to buy the dump," I shrieked.

He looked at me like I was a madwoman. "Who?"

"Isn't this house just like the one we were going to build?"

"Yes," he conceded.

"I'll bet the builder of this home will want to build another one like it on our lot. He's going to buy it. I just know it. Let's get him on the phone and have him meet us at the old house."

The next day I had the enrollment conversation of my life. Taking the builder into the kitchen, I pointed out the window to show him the million-dollar view. "Won't this make a stunning kitchen?" I asked. He nodded. Leading him out on the deck, I said, "Can't you imagine this fabulous view from the new master bedroom that you're going to build?"

Within fifteen minutes, he simply said, "I'll take it." I wanted to bless him, his children, and his grandchildren, but all I said was, "Good choice." He was a man with a vision, he saw potential and knew it was a fine deal. Because he bought it without a realtor, I actually made a profit. We used that money to pay down the new mortgage, until we were paying about the same amount as we had been paying for the dump—and we were living in the Dream Palace!

The life-changing lesson I learned was to trust myself and my dreams. With one single step, you are no longer just talking about your dream, but rather acting on it. New resources and opportunities show up that were not available when you were just thinking about it. The builder would have never been a prospect if I had not had the trust in myself and in life to first say yes to my dream. There were no promises, guarantees, or assurances—and aren't those the times when our faith is really tested? True faith comes from acting on what you believe, what really matters to you, on the dreams of your heart. I don't know any other way to build self-trust then to risk everything for a dream and follow through on it, no matter what anyone else says.

What happens when you don't trust is that things get difficult, blocked, stuck, or might even fall apart. You start to doubt—first your decisions, and eventually everything. You might start to compromise on your dream, and try to manipulate the situation. In your best attempt to control the outcome, you might be the one who unknowingly sabotages it.

Just Trust

Remember, the key when you are in the midst of doubt is not to push that voice away, but to turn toward it and pay attention. Listen to your fears, concerns, and second thoughts. But don't run with them. Take a moment to regain your clarity. Ask yourself: "What is real?" Better yet, write it out, and write out what you're thinking or telling yourself about this. What stories are you making up that might be disempowering your dream? What are you not trusting and why? How can you move this obstacle, this mistrust or lack of trust, out of your way? Get clear about what you don't trust, get to the heart of your lack of faith. If you don't get to the bottom of it, it might cost you your dream.

Ask yourself what you can do to learn to trust, or let go of your lack of trust. Letting go happens when you have clarity about what you want, you've done everything there is to do, and now you can relax. Stop controlling, holding back, fretting, or worrying. *Just trust.* Two simpler words might never have been spoken; when it comes to your dream, there is nothing more profound. It's a critical component for creating a life of joy and ease. Here are some questions you can use to examine your relationship to trust:

- Do you trust yourself and others?

- Do you trust the process, your environment, the universe, the timing?

- Do you trust that your dream will come true?

- What actions are you taking to demonstrate that you do trust?

Trust is a giant obstacle for many people. If you don't have it, you'll have to find it, and you'll have to practice trusting yourself above all. Trust the decisions you make, and believe that you're entitled to want your dream and to realize it. Trust comes first; that's what allows the extraordinary results to show up. But trust is critical all the way through the process as well—when you confront setbacks, when you come upon unexpected opportunities or changes of plan, and even when all your dreams come true. *Just trust.*

Being Balanced

One of the ways to develop trust in yourself and the things around you is to keep yourself healthy by being centered and balanced. Feeling good about yourself leads to greater self-confidence, which is one of the places that trust comes from. You are a product of what you eat, how you live, how you rest and recreate, and what you think. All of these things filter into how you feel about yourself and, ultimately, what you allow yourself to trust.

You can work at achieving balance by incorporating some relaxation exercises into your life. The secret is to take it at your own pace, doing activities with which you feel comfortable. Take a few deep, cleansing breaths before you start a new task; closing your eyes and concentrating on your breath will allow you to feel more centered. By "being here and now" you stay connected with your life, and your passion. This is not about designing a five-year plan for yourself, and then spending another five years figuring out how to control your life and make it happen. It's not about having it all happen right now.

It's giving yourself some leeway about what you want, trusting the timing and the process, and being in action in some way each day on the things you love to do. It's really quite simple.

The element that's critical to making the timing work in your life is to *be present*, to be here, right now, enjoying and living your life. What could you change or create right now that would make a difference? You don't have to restructure your entire life this minute; maybe breathing deeply is all you need right now. Sometimes it's a matter of life or breath. Are you too busy to breathe?

Take a fresh page in your Dream Book, and list the things you will start doing today for yourself to help achieve and maintain balance in your life. These can be simple things: taking an extra five minutes in the morning to stretch and relax, or spending thirty minutes at the end of the day journaling and feeling gratitude. Decide what you can do that will keep you centered and balanced in the following areas:

- At home

- At work

- With others

- Alone

In the Flow

Being in the flow means that the timing of your life is working for you, that there's a level of synchronicity where things seem to happen. Synchronicity is when things start to happen at the right time, flow together easily, and work interchangeably. One of my clients spoke to me of his dream to be featured in the local newspaper. The next day he called to tell me that the paper, seemingly out of the blue, wanted to interview him.

Surprises happen when you're living in the flow; you can get in sync with the universe when you learn to trust yourself and life, when you're not so busy trying to control and manipulate everything. Slow down and relax, let go of some of your resistance, and things will seem to happen naturally.

Michelle decided that it was important for her business that she travel to Florida once a month, but she didn't know how she could work it into her budget. The next day a travel agency called to say that her name had been selected out of a random drawing, and that she'd won six round-trip tickets to Florida. Since then, the trips have proven so fruitful that she is considering relocating to Florida.

Recently, I decided to hire a personal assistant. The next day, after I presented a workshop in San Francisco, a young woman came up to me and said, "If you ever need a personal assistant, I would be interested in working for you." I hadn't even announced it. She started the following week.

Michelle's experience, winning the round-trip Florida tickets, was pure synchronicity. She had done nothing to put herself in that particular path; it just happened. I was clear about what I wanted and I believe things like this happen all the time. Maybe that's why they do. This is by no means a trivial component of making your dreams come true; letting go of the doubt and fear, and being open to greater ease, is a critical part of the process.

The Ability to Discern

When life brings you wonderful surprises, as it inevitably will, you might begin to be concerned that you'll have too many things coming at you too fast. After all, if you enroll people in your dream, others will start trying to enroll you in theirs. As more and more possibilities become evident, how will you know when to say yes and when to say no?

Again, *just trust.* Here are some simple questions to guide you in the process of trusting, in determining whether or not any particular job, activity, meeting or relationship is right for you:

- Is this what I want to do now?

- Is this part of my dream?

- Is this something I'm passionate or excited about?

You'll often know the right answer; it generally comes automatically. You'll know when you're excited about something, or when it seems like a duty. Don't be afraid to affix labels: "This is something I feel obligated to do." If that's the way you feel, you might let that project go. Other more passion-provoking opportunities are available. In fact the possibilities are unlimited as long as you honor yourself. Follow what has heart and meaning for you. Be willing to say yes; be willing to say, "I'll think about it;" and be willing to say, "No, thank you!" This is an essential skill to cultivate.

As you move forward with your dreams, the ability to discern between what you do and don't want is very important. At one point on my journey, I developed a very simple practice that I used for myself. What I wanted, at that time in my life, was to open to more of my feminine, essential self. For the first part of my professional career, I had been driven by more masculine energies—I was much more ambitious and driven than I am now. The pivotal turning point for me was the moment when I got clear that what mattered to me more than almost anything was my quality of life.

Rather than trying to please everyone, I got more discerning about how I wanted to use my time, because there's only a limited amount of it that anyone of us has. The "no more, now what?" practice was an important tool, but I also needed a tool for discerning what I *did* want. So I created a filter. I asked myself, what simple criteria need to be in place in order to say "yes" to an opportunity? Remember, what I wanted was to open to more of my feminine self, so I came up with an acronym, FEM. In order for me to say yes to a professional opportunity, it had to be Fun, Easy and Make Money. In order for me to say yes to an altruistic or nonprofit opportunity, it needed to be Fulfilling, Energizing, and Meaningful. And in basic day-to-day existence, it was about Food, Exercise, and Meditation. I'm making light of this, but it was completely life-changing. If you can identify a shortlist of criteria that need to be in place for you to say "yes," and then really hold true to it, you're going to get back so much more time and energy to apply to the dreams that truly matter to you as well as discover your authentic "Yes."

The more you trust yourself and your own ability to make choices based on your passion, the more easily and effortlessly life will organize around you. Trust is the secret to remaining balanced and centered as you move into greater uncertainty in pursuit of your dreams.

CHAPTER 15
Hear Life's Dream For You

Not all those who wander are lost.

—J.R.R. Tolkien

Since page one of this book, we've focused on you and your dream. Now we're going to turn a corner. The goal of this chapter is to inspire you to dream bigger—to go beyond what you've chosen so far. There's the dream you have for life, and then there's the dream that life has for you. As we come to the end of this book, I'd like you to open yourself up to the latter.

Think of a dream that will be a gift to the world. A dream that will touch, inspire, and impact—maybe even leave a legacy. Write down a dream that you don't even know how to accomplish. What is the dream you must accomplish in order to die happy and fulfilled?

If you want to live every day with passion, I recommend that you come up with a dream and design a project that's bigger than your life, one that you don't know how to achieve. Don't create a project "out of the blue," develop one out of your purpose as you would any other project. My bigger-than-life project is that, by the time I die, people will be speaking about dreams in a completely new way, as if their dreams are something that absolutely can be had by a specific day. When you speak to me about your dreams, be prepared to pull out your calendar. I'm interested in getting you into action to make your dreams real.

I'm not yet certain how to fulfill my bigger-than-life project, but it turns me on and gets me into conversations with extraordinary people. Remember, my dream is to partner with creative visionaries to produce impactful results. Speaking with people about their dreams allows everyone to show up as a visionary, to be fully excited about their ideas. I don't allow myself to be stopped by the fact that I haven't figured out how to accomplish my bigger-than-life project. I move on by developing strategies and steps, by scheduling it into my life, and letting life happen. And it does.

Once you're clear about what you're committed to, incredible resources, possibilities, and people will show up to help you. Although it might not be completed during your lifetime, it will allow you to play an extraordinary game. You will definitely feel passion.

Imagine having the dream of a loving world that works or of creating heaven on earth in your own special way. There have been many big dreamers before you—the names we all know, like Mother Teresa or Gandhi, but also everyday people like us who make a significant contribution to the world. Pursuing your big dream is not only about doing what you say or what you want; it's actually about being and becoming a different kind of person.

Where do you begin? In what area are you committed to making a difference? Are you committed to a planet that's clean and healthy? A man I know has a big dream to ensure that the rainforest is still in existence when his children's children are grown. Maybe your interest is in the area of health and medicine. How about a cure for cancer or AIDS in your lifetime? Perhaps your contribution will be in the area of education or communications?

Anselm Rothschild, a personal friend, had a very big dream. He was committed to ending hunger in the world, and he dedicated his life to doing it. He chose to pursue his dream by composing music and producing events that promoted global peace and an end to hunger. During the 1960s, Anselm organized the Freedom from Hunger Foundation's first walkathon, which became the prototype for fundraising walkathons across the country. He didn't stop there, however. While Anselm had lots of credits and credentials, he is probably best remembered as the head writer and coordinating producer of the educational components of the *LiveAid* fundraising concert and telecast. Anselm was a man who followed his dream. Although he tragically died before the age of forty, what a life he lived and what a legacy he left! His contribution made a specific and measurable difference to billions of people. Anselm's message raised awareness of the problem to a new level through *LiveAid*, which was broadcast worldwide to one hundred and sixty countries.

Whatever your big dream is, this is an opportunity for you to get into action on it. If you don't think you are the kind of person who can start a foundation or a movement, perhaps you are the type who can volunteer at such an organization. Look around. Start with what you're passionate about, what matters to you, what moves you. As you're watching television or surfing the internet, notice what gets you excited, what angers you, what touches your heart. Those are good places to begin.

Talk with people who are already involved in an issue that you feel passionate about and learn how you can participate. Make a contribution. Make a promise and then take action to fulfill your promise; that's what your life is about.

The critical thing is to begin. One thing will lead to another. You'll know when it feels right, and the personal feeling of satisfaction and fulfillment will be beyond description. Perhaps all we want from our lives is to make a difference.

The True Meaning of Wealth

I researched the origin of the word "wealth" and made an amazing discovery. The modern definition is, "the abundance of valuable resources or material possessions." But this excludes the core meaning as held in the originating Old English word *weal*, which is from an Indo-European word stem. In this larger understanding of wealth, an individual, community, region, or country that possesses an abundance of such possessions or resources to the benefit of the common good is known as wealthy. It was about shared resources, about looking out for and helping each other. It was about generosity or commonwealth.

Contrary to the modern definition, wealth is not about how much you are worth or how much you own, but instead, true wealth is about how much your gifts, possessions, and resources benefit the common good. The challenge is that everyone is looking for how to quantify wealth in the same way we measure sugar, gold, or a sack of potatoes. Unlike money, wealth is not something you quantify with a scale or bank statement.

How do we as visionaries, change-agents, messengers, leaders, and businesses achieve this true wealth and become a voice and a force for transformation? The true measurement of wealth is the amount of meaning you create for yourself, for the people you care about, and the world around us. We know there's no equality when it comes to the distribution of monetary wealth. When we come together, however, as a community, team, or group around a shared goal, vision, or dream, we certainly can have a bigger impact. And regardless of what's going on in the economy, I encourage you to adopt the dream of becoming a wealthy person. The measure of true wealth is living a joyful and meaningful life, including creating, pursuing, and achieving dreams that are aligned with your purpose. And these dreams come in all flavors, colors, and shapes. No dream is too big or too small. The question is, "What's meaningful to you?"

My client Mike Murphy, who was a successful car dealer, had everything he ever dreamed of in the way of material wealth, but he still felt unfulfilled. Then one day, he met the woman of his dreams, Margot, and fell deeply in love. Mike thought his life was complete, until one day he found a lump in Margot's breast. She was diagnosed with cancer, and for the next nine years, Mike fought to keep his beloved wife, and his dream, alive. When she passed away in 2011, he thought his life was over too. In the depths of despair, with no reason to keep going, he answered a call from a friend who asked for his help: his sister-in-law, Amanda, had breast cancer and needed a referral to a doctor. Not only did Mike make the referral; he went along to the appointment. "I'll never forget the day," he said. "The doctor gave Amanda a grim prognosis: there was no hope of her beating the cancer, but with aggressive treatment, she had the opportunity to extend her life for a few more months. Amanda was a single mom with three small children, and would fight for every extra day she could spend with them. Seeing her resolve, the doctor told us that the best protocol for her would be a combination of three types of chemotherapy. And then he said something that Margot and I had never heard, in all our years of battling cancer: "'Unfortunately, your insurance will only pay for one, so that is all I can give you.'"

In that moment, it dawned on Mike how much Margot's journey had been eased by his wealth. "It was almost embarrassing to realize it only now," he recalls. "Without even thinking, I handed the doctor my credit card and told him to give Amanda whatever she needed." And that spontaneous gesture became the seed of a new purpose in Mike's life, a big dream that gave him a new reason to live and honored the memory of his beloved wife. "I now knew what I was here to do: to learn how to give and serve others and make a difference in the lives of people like Amanda who were not only fighting cancer but fighting a daily battle to put food on the table, keep a roof over their families' heads, or pay their medical bills," he says. Mike started the Love From Margot Foundation, which has helped more than one hundred low-income women in Oakland and the San Francisco Bay area who have been diagnosed with cancer, providing financial support and education. Mike's big dream is a world where no woman with cancer has to lose precious time with her family because of a lack of resources.

An Unstoppable Dream

My friend Cynthia Kersey is a woman with a big dream. And it's a dream that came out of one of the greatest wounds of her life. "Who knew that when my husband of twenty years and I separated, my pain would open the door to my greatest purpose?" she reflects. Faced with spending the holidays alone, Cynthia decided rather than feel sorry for herself, she would dedicate herself to doing something for someone else.

She called her mentor and friend Millard Fuller, the founder of Habitat for Humanity International. He said, "Cynthia, when you have a great pain in your life, you need a greater purpose." He told her about his recent visit to Nepal, one of the poorest nations in the world, and suggested that building a house for a Nepalese family in need could be a great project for her.

As she sat with his suggestion, she asked herself, "How many houses would I need to build that would be bigger than this pain in my life?" When she finally got to the number one hundred, that felt bigger than her pain. Although she'd never been to Nepal and had no idea how to pull something like this off, she felt invigorated by that greater purpose and grateful to have something to take her mind off of herself and her problems.

A year later, she had raised two hundred thousand dollars and brought a team of eighteen people to Nepal and they built the first three of the one hundred houses that would get built over the following year. Over the next few years she continued to engage in all sorts of philanthropic projects while running her business, until finally, in 2006, she discovered the big dream that would change her life: education. Talking to mothers in the developing world, she noted that, "their greatest concern and their greatest hope was how to get their children an education. Because without it, nothing would change and their children would have little hope to do more than to eke out a meager existence for themselves and their families." Something clicked. "I couldn't imagine what it would be like if my child would never learn how to read or write his name, count money, or have no hope of an inspiring future," she says. "Suddenly, I became clear about the reason I'd been drawn halfway around the world, and a dream birthed within me that I could not ignore. I knew I had to help. I was shocked by number of children who were denied access to the basic human right of even a primary education. That is where I decided I would focus. There was just one problem. I had no idea what to do."

Cynthia did not let that stop her. After all, this was a woman who had written a book called *Unstoppable*—now was the time for her to live up to that name. When her birthday came around, instead of receiving gifts she held a fundraiser and raised enough money to help build two schools in Uganda.

"It was hugely inspiring to know that we were changing the lives of every child who would attend those schools for generations to come," she recalls, "but that night also changed my life. I initially thought

I was doing something great for these children, but I realized that supporting them was doing something great for me, and for everyone who attended. That unusual birthday party was the greatest gift of my life, and an even greater purpose emerged within me to do a whole lot more."

The dream that was born that night became the Unstoppable Foundation—a nonprofit that has, in just a few short years, helped over seven thousand children in three countries in Africa to receive an education every day, through a proven model called "Sponsor a Village." Partnering with other organizations and the local communities, the Unstoppable Foundation not only builds schools but also provides access to clean water and sanitation, food and nutrition, healthcare, and income and empowerment training for parents to more than twenty-five thousand community members.

The results, as Cynthia describes it, are "thriving communities with the tools to help them stop the cycle of poverty in their villages." This year, she celebrated the graduation of the first class of girls from the secondary school they built, the first in the region.

I was there in the early days encouraging Cynthia to let go of her traditional career and start the Unstoppable Foundation, and I am very proud to have continued to support her work by serving on her Board and funding her foundation. Dream University® has sponsored several villages in the Ngosuani Community of the Maasai Mara, contributing to the building of schools, in addition to providing all the other critical resources to the entire community.

One of the things that I find so deeply moving about Cynthia's work is this: Imagine living in a community where one day it's hard to even get pencils and then, only a year later, day you're attending a local version of Dream University®, a place where you are given the tools and resources to create the life you want. That's a dream I want to support in any way I can!

Another way that I am supporting dreaming in the school system is through an initiative that's closer to home. I recently learned about an organization called the Future Project, founded by Yale University graduates Kanya Balakrishna and Andrew Mangino. They observed that many conversations around what needed to change in the world came back to the education system, but most people were missing what they saw as the real problem: the kids were "bored, uninspired, and didn't see how what they were learning in the classroom was connected to their lives and dreams outside of school." Balakrishna and Mangino came up with the idea of bringing dreaming back into education. And the way they do it is by dispatching full-time Dream Directors to work in high schools, helping the kids learn to connect with their passions and create big dreams. I love this project and am exploring multiple ways that I can support and collaborate with them. They've now worked with more than 5000 students and are continuing to expand.

My Big Dream

A few years ago, I knew there was a big new dream that was trying to come through me, and that if I didn't take some time to stop and empty, as we've talked about, it wouldn't have a chance to surface, much less be developed and created. So I went to my calendar and I crossed out the Christmas week. Suddenly my hand crossed out all of December. I remember thinking, "how could I possibly take a month off?" But I did. And it turned out that was just the beginning for me.

The next three years turned into a Passion Quest. I still had to work, I still had responsibilities and bills to pay, so what wasn't like my whole life was on hold, but I was in a very important time of emptying, saying "no more," being more discerning—practicing everything we've talked about so far in the book. Throughout the process, I kept asking: "What's the big dream? What's the next level of my work and development?" Every time I got a great idea, or even a not-so-great idea, I put it in a book called My Book of Ideas. In that book was everything from "go work for a colleague" to "get a corporate job," "move to Fiji," "write another book," "retire," and so on.

I had to restrain myself from turning any one idea into a strategy and acting upon it. It was quite a crucible for me, allowing this dream to come forward. But by not acting on any of them, I built up a dynamic tension and one day, all at once, my big dream appeared, intact and complete. I saw that I was meant to create something called The Meaning Institute. It is designed to be a modern-day mystery school. You're probably wondering what that means—well, it's about studying the mysteries of life, the things that cannot be seen and touched, like love, compassion, power, and passion. I designed a one-year curriculum that included four weekends of initiations through which people awaken to the depth of who they are and cross over a threshold into living a more meaningful life.

I wasn't certain if I would ever do it again, but after completing the first year, I can tell you hands-down that it was but the most transformational year of my life. It felt divinely guided and inspired. I was able to trust myself enough and be trusted enough by one hundred individuals to create something truly unique, extraordinary, and meaningful. I'm happy to say that now that I know what I'm doing, I definitely intend to do it again. The level of healing, awakening, growth, and community that came out of it was unparalleled for me. The bottom line is, through following my big dream I learned to live on a much deeper level, and from that everything in my life has changed.

12 Ways to Be a Twenty-First Century Visionary

As you begin to consider yourself wealthy, I'd also encourage you to consider yourself a visionary. As we discussed in chapter seven, if you turn the voice of the Doubter down you'll find the voice of the Realist, and if you turn up the voice of the Dreamer, you'll hear the voice of the Visionary. This voice rarely concerns itself with details. Think of people like Steve Jobs or Richard Branson. When a visionary gets bogged down with minutia it can impact the big vision and ideas.

As previously stated, a visionary is someone who has a vision, speaks about it clearly, and shares it passionately. And since a true visionary has mastered enrollment, they rarely go it alone.

I am honored to be a member of the prestigious Transformational Leadership Council (TLC), a collaborative community of visionaries. Among my peers, those who appear the most successful (and happiest) have a value, as I do, on continual growth and development.

I often go on a Passion Quest, which I described in chapter three, taking the time to ask good questions and listen patiently for wisdom and answers. My last three years have been a period of soul searching, a time of creating, and a time to dream. I've learned to slow down and wait for guidance and in the empty space, this revelatory and relevant message emerged.

A Twenty-First Century Visionary:

1. **Has tremendous integrity.** Beyond keeping her agreements with herself and others, she answers to a higher Source. She is aligned with her values and usually has a mission, vision, calling, and dreams in many areas of life.

2. **Is comfortable with uncertainty, the place where true creation occurs.** He knows we were created to create and allows the time and space for this to occur. He understands that there is deep knowing under uncertainty but he appreciates the value of not knowing.

3. **Has extraordinary faith.** She is able to act on what's important to her even without assurance and guarantees. She can walk on faith without knowing the strategy or even clear next steps.

4. **Knows that the secret to enlightenment is to relax.** As he relaxes, his ego (with its agenda, fears, and doubts) can slip away or get quiet, allowing for peace. He is left with his essential self, Essence, or soul.

5. **Practices getting empty in order to hear the voice of your inner wisdom and feel its presence.** She often creates rituals and sacred spaces as ways to invite this in.

6. **Can consciously drop into a deeper place of wisdom, knowing, and truth, and can ideate/dream, and speak from this place.**

7. **Is aware that miracles happen in their own time and is able to wait rather than asserting his will or effort too soon.** He trusts the process enough to let it unfold. He can have a strong intention, yet hold it spaciously.

8. **Is receptive and knows that "give and take" is not the same as "give and receive" and that giving and receiving need to be done in balance.** She practices restraint, allowing space for true creation and original thought to happen.

9. **Does not live primarily as a problem solver, but more as a creative force.** He is aware that it is more powerful to move toward what he wants than away from what he doesn't want, yet he knows that both creation and destruction serve.

10. **Has a conscious relationship with the silent witness, the part that can see many points of view, all sides and new perspectives.** As a big dreamer, she uses her imagination to traverse new terrain.

11. **Knows when to be collaborative and when to be hierarchal.** He has the courage, clarity, and commitment to share dreams and ideas and empower others to take ownership.

12. **Is crucial to the Dream Movement's ultimate dream, which is to make the world a more whole and abundant place.** She knows that with one single highly intentional step, the world can, has, and will continue to change.

We are all twenty-first-century visionaries with important work to do as we heal, awaken, and transform. As we learn to dream, we can create a truly beautiful world. It is time.

EPILOGUE
The Beginning

Although this is the last chapter of the book, it is only the beginning for you—the beginning of your dream-come-true life. Your dreams are the expression of your heart and soul. Get in touch with what matters to you most. Bring more of who you are and what you love into your everyday life. This is your life, and although life is short, how we live it, each and every day, is what will make it joyful and fulfilling.

Remember that the formula to DREAM is:

1. Clarify your dream—define what you truly want and get it out of your head.

2. Believe in your dream—remove the obstacles, especially your doubts, fears, and limiting beliefs.

3. Act on your dream. Design the projects, strategies, and steps to make it happen.

And of course, always remember that your #1 shortcut step is to share your dreams with others and enroll them as part of your team. Ask people to help you and ask how you can help them achieve their dreams.

Standing in your purpose, you can see your dreams with great clarity and commit to having them. Use your resources, the ones you know about right now and the ones you will make available to yourself. Allow yourself to be imaginative and inventive, to create projects that move you forward.

Design your internal and external environments so that they are nurturing to your dreams and to the projects that will make your dreams real. Trust the process, the synchronicity in the universe and, most of all, trust yourself. You are, and you can be, as imaginative and resourceful as you need to be; get in action to live the life you love. Remember, you are a dreamer at heart with the freedom to create what you want.

Share your dream with others; the process will help you enroll people who will want to contribute time, money, energy, and other resources to support you. When you can envision it, you will be able to speak about your dream in a way that generates excitement, enthusiasm, and powerful results.

Be unstoppable. You can have the life you want, the one that works for you. The possibilities are all waiting for you to make your life the extraordinary experience it is meant to be.

Simply DREAM!

About the Author

Marcia Wieder, CEO of Dream University® and Founder of The Meaning Institute, is a thought leader on visionary thinking. She is known for her unique blend of depth and levity and her ability to bridge inner and outer concepts in a practical and entertaining style.

With over thirty years of speaking, training, and coaching experience, Marcia has touched audiences of 80-8000 people, for corporations such as AT&T, Gap, and American Express, as well as entrepreneurial organizations. Whether teaching at the Stanford Business School, speaking to executives in China, or addressing young women at Girl Scout Camps, her riveting message has a worldwide impact.

Appearing several times on *Oprah, The Today Show,* and in her own PBS-TV special, Marcia is a bestselling author of 15 books, all dedicated to achieving your dreams. As past president of the National Association of Women Business Owners, she was regularly invited to the White House where she assisted three former U.S. presidents, Ronald Reagan, Jimmy Carter, and George Bush Sr.

She was also able to further spread her passion for dreaming as a columnist for the *San Francisco Chronicle* and *Huffington Post,* where she urges readers to take "The Great Dream Challenge." As a pioneer in the coaching industry, she developed a methodology and has certified Dream Coaches® worldwide, who are bringing her work to battered women's shelters, prisons, and corporations. She lives in California where she is pursuing her dream of living near the water and balancing work and play, with much more emphasis on play.

Marcia gives speeches and inspiring workshops on dream achievement, team building, and visionary thinking. Her most requested titles include:

Dreaming Is Serious Business

Real Results through Visionary Leadership

Tapping Innovation & Creativity

Passion and Productivity

Create Your Dream Life: On Your Way in Just One Day

With Meaning Life Makes Sense

If you would like to know more, please call: 415-381-5564 or visit her speaker website:

MarciaWieder.com

DREAM UNIVERSITY®

Dream University® is the only university in the world solely dedicated to helping you discover and achieve your personal and professional dreams. Our results-oriented courses, inspiring faculty, supportive community, and networking provide practical resources to take action toward success on your own terms.

Dream University® has an online campus in order to fulfill its mission to teach millions of people worldwide how to achieve their dreams. Regardless of your location or socioeconomic status, Dream University® will provide you with its proven methods, tools, and world class faculty to help you identify and achieve your dreams.

Dream University® is for you if:

- You want to create and realize an important personal or professional dream.

- You desire new clarity and resources for the 21st century.

- You want to express your voice as a visionary or leader.

- You dare to dream big!

This curriculum will help you:

- Live a more meaningful life.

- Gain clarity about what you do and don't want.

- Remove any and all obstacles.

- Get "into action" on the dreams that matter to you.

Visit: www.DreamUniversity.com

A Thank You Gift for Being a Fellow Dreamer

These powerful tools are designed to help you dream big and succeed.

Feel free to share them with friends and family.

www.DreamUniversity.com/gift

ENDNOTES

1 Jean Houston, *The Search for the Beloved: Journeys in Mythology and Sacred Psychology,* (Tarcher, 1997) p. 112

2 *ibid,* p. 108

3 Wayne Dyer, *Your Sacred Self* (HarperCollins, 1995) p. 178

4 Joseph Joubert, *The Notebooks of Joseph Joubert,* (NYRB Classics, 2005) p. 24

5 William Blake, *The Marriage of Heaven and Hell* (Oxford Classics, 1975) p. xvii

6 Audre Lorde, Joan Wylie Hall, *Conversations with Audre Lorde* (University Press of Mississippi, 2004) p. 91